CHRISTIANITY AND THE STATE

BY

WILLIAM TEMPLE

BISHOP OF MANCHESTER

*Being the Henry Scott Holland Memorial
Lectures delivered in Liverpool in
January and February* 1928

MACMILLAN AND CO., LIMITED
ST. MARTIN'S STREET, LONDON
1928

CHRISTIANITY AND THE STATE

MACMILLAN AND CO., Limited
LONDON · BOMBAY · CALCUTTA
MADRAS · MELBOURNE

THE MACMILLAN COMPANY
NEW YORK · BOSTON · CHICAGO
DALLAS · SAN FRANCISCO

THE MACMILLAN CO. OF CANADA, Ltd.
TORONTO

TO

MY FRIEND

R. H. TAWNEY

PREFACE

THE invitation to deliver the Henry Scott Holland Memorial Lectures in 1928 produced in me a strong conflict of feeling. I wished to accept it, partly because of my deep interest in the problem with which in one or other of its phases the Lecturer is to be concerned— " the theology of the Incarnation and its bearing on the social and economic life of man "—partly because of my profound admiration for the man whom they commemorate. It is impossible to exaggerate the service rendered to the cause of Christian civilisation by his zeal, his width of sympathy, his glowing eloquence, his comprehensive philosophy. It is deeply to be regretted that he nowhere brought together the architectonic principles of his thought. They have to be disentangled from prophetic utterances on a great variety of subjects. But those who have sought to penetrate his secret have learnt that behind all the fervour of feeling and the riot of words there was a massive and coherent philosophical theology. It may be one function of the Memorial Lectureship that through it minds in some real sympathy with his should present the intellectual grounds for the faith and hope which he kindled in so many. The invitation to take part in that endeavour was hardly to be refused.

On the other hand, I knew that all I could offer would be sketchy and amateurish. The first Lectures given on this Foundation set a standard to deter the most shameless, and I trembled to think of my sporadic reflections appearing side by side with Mr. Tawney's *Religion and the Rise of Capitalism.* Moreover, I had the good fortune to hear part of the second course, delivered by the Rev. C. E. Osborne, and the memory of it deepened the sense of my incompetence.

But I reflected that, while their work will for many years be invaluable to students, there was need also for such brief expositions as might stimulate those, who are not and cannot be specialists, to think with close attention about this great theme. Perhaps there was a place in the series for a Lecturer who knows no more about the subject than any educated man or woman could know at the end of five years or thereabouts, without giving more time to it than anyone could give who cared enough. Consequently I would ask all readers to treat this book as a provocation to thought and to further reading, not as conveying instruction to be absorbed.

It is, therefore, not only by way of acknowledging my debt, though that is an obvious duty, but also by way of indicating a possible course of reading, that I mention the more or less contemporary works to which I have chiefly had recourse for the purposes of these Lectures. They are the following :

Tawney, R. H., *Religion and the Rise of Capitalism*.
Pollock, Sir F., *History of the Science of Politics*.
Murray, R. H., *The History of Political Science from Plato to the Present*.
Duff, J. A., *Spinoza's Political and Ethical Philosophy*.
Figgis, J. N., *From Gerson to Grotius*.
—— *Churches in the Modern State.*
Green, T. H., *Principles of Political Obligation.*
Laski, H. J., *The Problem of Sovereignty*.
—— *A Defence of Liberty against Tyrants : a translation of the Vindiciæ contra Tyrannos by Junius Brutus, with an Historical Introduction by Harold J. Laski*.
MacIver, R. M., *Community*.
—— *The Modern State.*

Unwin, G., *Studies in Economic History: the Collected Papers of George Unwin; edited with an Introductory Memoir by R. H. Tawney.*

Of these I should wish especially to commend the first and the two last on the list. For I believe that the most important problems to which we have to devote our attention are two : What is the bearing of Religion on the economic structure of society with which we are familiar ? and What is the relation of the State to Society or the Community ?

W. Manchester.

CONTENTS

CHRISTIANITY AND THE STATE

LECTURE I

ONE of the most prominent features of recent religious history has been the steadily increasing effort to recover something like a real Christian sociology. It was not till shortly before the Reformation that constructive work on this subject came to an end, and the Reformation itself in some of its phases re-vitalised for a time the waning interest of religion in this field. The long story has been set out with wide knowledge and splendid eloquence by my predecessor in this Lecture-ship, Mr. R. H. Tawney, whose book on *Religion and the Rise of Capitalism* has set for his successors a standard which must cover with confusion such amateurs of the subject as myself when they are asked to appear in his company.

B   1

The revival of interest in the subject may similarly be traced in a volume lately published by the Student Christian Movement on *Christian Social Reformers of the Nineteenth Century*, edited by the Rev. Hugh Martin. It began as an expression of sheer sympathy with distress; but this sympathy soon led to an attack on certain elements in the accepted order of society, and when once such an attack in the name of Christianity had been made, there was no escape from the demand that the whole existing political and social order should be examined in the light of Christian principles. No such examination can be free from the influence proceeding from the predominant interests of the time, and the Christian Social Movement of the later nineteenth and quite early twentieth century— the movement with which the name of Henry Scott Holland is indissolubly associated—was mainly concerned with the economic aspect of the social order. That remains of vast importance; but two events in recent experience —the World War of 1914–1918 and our own so-called General Strike of 1926—have pressed upon us questions concerning the nature of

the social structure itself.   Accordingly I propose to direct attention in these Lectures to
the nature of the State, the grounds and
limits of its authority, its relation to the
welfare of citizens, and the relation of different
States to one another, seeking to understand
these as they are illuminated alike by Christian
principles and by the experience of which
History is the record.

We begin with some general considerations.
And first may I stress with all possible emphasis that there is no such thing as a Christian
social ideal, if by that is meant a pattern
constitution deducible from the Christian
Gospel, to which we ought to conform the
actual arrangements of our various states?
If Christianity committed itself to such an
ideal, it would be hard indeed to believe that
it is the absolute and universal religion.   Men
differ in temperament, in aspiration, in experience, and in political capacity, both widely
and fundamentally; it is very hard to suppose
that there is any one form of political structure
which they ought all to adopt, or even towards
which they ought all to be advancing.   Moreover, to construct an ideal is very different

from indicating the way of attaining it. Christianity offers something far more practical, far more immediately cogent, far more universally applicable, than an ideal; it offers principles, on which it is always possible to act forthwith, whatever the circumstances, and by following which men of different outlook will reach the best order for them, whatever that may turn out to be. And Christianity offers also the Power by which men may act on those principles.

It is impossible, as I think, to exaggerate the importance of this distinction between principles and ideals. Here we find the true reason why the Church must never commit itself to any kind of political programme or unite itself to any political party. For programmes and parties are inevitably concerned not only with principles but with particular methods of applying principles to a given situation; and about this men of equally complete Christian loyalty may diametrically differ; for the question is partly, and sometimes wholly, one of expediency and judgment. If we are concerned to establish an ideal, we may form a party to take the steps necessary

even here there is room
at certain points; but
llow and apply certain
e for contemporary
iples, that is, appre-
ies concerning human
s and circumstances
expect and tolerate
nd consequently of
come these as illus-
y of our principles;
arious may unite in
evidence tending to
y.

nt Christian sociology
ned upon what I now
nciples, if such a phrase
have myself been accus-
four of these as implicit
therefore as binding upon
ple. These are the sanctity
the fact of Fellowship, the
and the power of Sacrifice.[1]

atement of these my books *Christus*
, and *Personal Religion and the Life*
-68.

To these we are brought
is the Social Gospel, o
thing) what are the
Gospel, in relation t
of society. But they
mental of all; and
deeper questions af
society and the na
also have in our min
realities—God and

It is commonly s
great advance upon
Ethics from Politics.
two comments : the
in fact, separate them
the sense that he wro
Politics and other boo
if this separation was du
than himself he did not r
at all. And my second
whereas Plato had a perfe
believe a perfectly correct
the relation between them,
regarding them as different
unity, had yet no clear co
relation to each other. Ar

Aristotle's confusion is his omission of any reference to Immortality. For him that omission was inevitable, because, apparently, he did not believe in personal immortality. If we agree with him there, we must try, like him, to work out our theory of Man and the State on the hypothesis that the State survives the successive generations of its own citizens, and that the goal of human life is such perfection as may be attained before death ends our development. On that hypothesis the conflict of claims between those spiritual values which are irrelevant to the State, such as the attainment of the Vision of God on the part of one of its citizens, and those values which belong to the State and may be conserved by it for future generations, is likely to prove irreconcilable. For the individual Aristotle says that the highest aim is ἐφ' ὅσον ἐνδέχεται ἀθανατίζειν [1] (as far as may be to live the life immortal) or τὸν θεὸν θεωρεῖν καὶ θεραπεύειν [2] (to behold God and to serve Him); and this will only be possible to a civilised and educated man in the tranquillity of a well-ordered

[1] *Eth. Nic* X. 1177 *b*, 33.
[2] *Eth. Eud.* IV. 1249 *b*, 20.

society. Even so, it is only possible for the few; broadly speaking, the test of individual excellence is found in citizenship, while the test of political excellence—the excellence of a society—is found chiefly in its permanence.

But if we believe in Immortality, whether " conditional " or not, it at once affects all our perspectives, and Plato will guide us in the adjustment of them. It has been said of him that he sacrifices the individual to society. Nothing could be further from the truth. That false impression has arisen partly because people have taken his sketch of the Ideal City as a political programme, partly because they have not risen to the height of his austere morality. He does deprive the individual Guardian of much on which most of us set great value; but he does this because he believes it to be good for such an individual both in this life and in view of his immortal destiny. The City after all is for Plato in the last resort a school, educating us for the life to which we pass when school-days are over, and to which the entrance is death. We may disagree with the methods which he advocates for our discipline; we cannot, if we are

Christians, quarrel with the perspective in which he sets the issue.

Of course this is not to say that Plato would order society with a view to the immortality of the citizens in a way which would be mistaken if there were no such immortality in store for them. To suppose that would be to ignore his contention that the righteous life and order is best in itself as well as for its consequences, and would still be best in itself even if its consequences were nothing but suffering and defeat. What is true is that *The Republic* begins with a search for individual righteousness, and ends with a defence and picture of individual immortality, while the whole political argument occurs between these two. Moreover, it is declared that all constitutions spring from the moral standards adopted by the citizens; if the State is a Plutocracy, that is because the citizens give great honour to wealth, or at least allow great power to wealth; and the constitution then reproduces in the rising generation the scale of values from which it sprang, so that it is, for good or evil, the great moral educator. It is true that at one point Plato requires from some individuals—the Guardians—what is not, in his view, best for them as individuals, namely, that they shall leave the Beatific Vision to administer the State in the light of it; here for a moment, in his view, what is best for the individual clashes with what is best for the State; and the source of his trouble, as we shall see, is a defective conception of God. But even here, though what is asked of the Guardians is not ideally best for them, yet it is the best practicable in the circumstances; for if they refuse, they will be acting unrighteously, so the alternative is the worst fate that could befall them. Yet this requirement is only made of those whom the State itself has trained to virtue—only, therefore, of citizens in the Ideal City. In any actual society the wise man will keep out of politics, cowering as under a wall from the storm of evil influences with which society besets him, happy if he can escape unspotted to the other world.[1] So far is Plato from sacrificing the individual to the State.

Moreover, his analysis of the soul, and the corresponding structure of the State, is de-

[1] *Republic*, 496 *d*.

signed to illustrate the primary relationships in which individuals may stand to one another, and the proper relation between these relationships.[1]   A man may ignore his fellows; and so far as he acts from appetite alone, he does so.   If a thirsty man gives his cup of water to another saying, " Thy need is greater than mine," it is not his thirst which prompts him so to act.   Appetite, as such, ignores social relationships and social claims; but it must be satisfied if life is to be maintained. Secondly, a man may compete with his fellows, and Pride ($\theta\nu\mu\delta\varsigma$) expresses itself in such competition.   Thirdly, a man may co-operate with his fellows, all alike contributing to the general welfare, each content to make the contribution for which he is fitted; this is the expression of Reason.   These are the primary relationships possible between individuals.   Welfare depends on Reason, the Man, or distinctively human element in men, securing Pride as an ally in the control of Appetite; [2]   and the State is to be fashioned so as to express this scale of valuation and control, and to reproduce it in the characters

[1] *Republic*, 435 e–441 c.   [2] *Ibid.*, 588 c–589 b.

of successive generations of citizens. At every point for Plato the individual is the primary subject of concern.

No doubt he might have held this view even if he had not believed in Immortality. But it is the conviction that man is a denizen of Eternity as well as a citizen of a State which most of all emphasises his priority to the State, and this conviction we find Plato proclaiming as the climax of his work. For us at least that conviction must be pre-potent. We shall see as we go on some of the implications which it carries.

But first we must turn to that still more fundamental consideration which must lie at the root of any Christian sociology—the Being of God. In days when men discussed the Divine Right of Monarchs there was no danger of their omitting all reference to God in their political philosophy. But we must recognise that this was not so much due to any particular conviction on this subject as to a general habit of mind, which determined the method of approach to all subjects. In the flower of the Middle Ages philosophers had achieved a systematic unity of the whole of existing knowledge, under the reign of Theology, the Queen of Sciences, such as has never been repeated. Indeed the completeness of their success in their own period contributed to the greatness of the subsequent disruption. Just because the unification was so complete with regard to the existing field of knowledge, it exhibited a most unhealthy stability when the extension of knowledge began to call for modification or for reconstruction. Freedom for development in Art, in Science or in Politics could therefore only come by a total repudiation of the primacy of theology. This emancipation of the various departments of human activity is called the Renaissance. It led to a wonderful efflorescence in all directions. But it gained this result by departmentalising human life, so that its unity was totally destroyed. When the religious impulse set itself to break free from the system that cramped it no less disastrously than it cramped any other human activity, the departmentalising process was already an established fact; and though in many quarters, notably in Calvin's Geneva and in Knox's Scotland, the Reformation attempted to reassert the universal sway of religion, it increasingly accepted the view that religion is concerned with the individual soul in its relation to God, and should leave alone the political aspect of life. For a while the old vision lingered with reference to certain sides of life. The Puritans, heirs of the tradition of Calvin, seriously tried to revive it, and Baxter's *Directory* shows how late it could survive in undeniably Protestant circles. But religion had lost its controlling position before the Reformation, and the Reformation rather failed to recover it than threw it away.

For our purposes the significant name is that of Machiavelli. He has been execrated for preaching moral unscrupulousness. But his real importance is that he first expressed in a clear-cut form the emancipation of politics from the control of religion. He set political thought moving on the lines made familiar by Hobbes and Locke and Rousseau, lines which led through the total secularisation of politics to the deification of the State by Hegel and his school.

Now this movement of thought was by no means merely false; no great movement ever is. The mediæval structure was so inelastic that it prepared the way for a general break-up. The movement which started at the Renaissance, being emphatically a reaction and an emancipation, was almost as intolerant of the school of thought from which it broke away as that school was to the newer movements for which it could not make room within itself. The Enlightenment of the eighteenth century was as narrow in its antipathy to the Catholic tradition as ever that tradition had shown itself towards the early growth of science. The intolerance of rationalists is quite as deep as that of traditionalists, and if its weapon is contempt rather than persecution, that is at once more irritating to the victim and far more spiritually corrupting to him who indulges in it. But if there was real excuse for both parties to the quarrel in those days, there is none for us if we ignore the lessons of their history; and that we shall do if, in our attempt to revive the intimacy of connection that once obtained between religion and politics, we refuse to learn from all the profound and massive thinking that has been given to politics as a purely secular study.

There is, indeed, one great philosopher who, as I hope to show, can guide us to the right method of approach : I mean Spinoza, of whom it has been said that, accepting the starting-point of Machiavelli, he reached the conclusions of St. Augustine.

Spinoza had little influence on the thought of his day and is not a link in the chain of development which we shall briefly trace in the next Lecture. I propose, therefore, to take this opportunity of calling attention to the main positions of a thinker whom I esteem so highly, though there is hardly one of those positions which I could adopt precisely as Spinoza stated them. It is his temper and method of approach that seem to me so valuable.

It may appear paradoxical in an attempt to make a contribution to modern Christian sociology to suggest as a motto—Back to Spinoza. Spinoza died in 1677, and a great deal has happened since then both in the world of politics and in the world of philosophy. Moreover, he was not a Christian; and the question whether it is more accurate to say that he did not believe in God or to say that

he did not believe in anything else is likely to
agitate his commentators from time to time
so long as men read and think. But I wish
to call special attention to his two political
treatises, because they seem to me to supply
the best starting-point of any modern inquiry.
I do indeed regard Spinoza as the one modern
philosopher who is worthy to be named in the
same breath with Plato; and if his Politics
are a less overwhelming achievement than his
Ethics, they are also free from the defect or
obscurity of thought, whichever it be, which
gives rise to the agitating question already
mentioned. Let me say a word or two about
that defect, as I think it, and so leave clear
the way for a brief tribute to Spinoza's
greatness.

It is, I think, true that Spinoza is involved
in a tension amounting to a contradiction
between a refusal to acknowledge any divine
transcendence in the full sense of the term
and a glowing religious experience which could
really be satisfied with nothing else. The
austere but burning aspiration of the fifth
book of his Ethics is really inconsistent with
the account of the Divine Nature given in

c

the first, though technically the definition of God is wide enough for anything. " God is an absolutely infinite Being, that is, substance consisting of infinite attributes; *Per Deum intelligo ens absolute infinitum, hoc est substantiam constantem infinitis attributis.*" [1] This ought to have led him at least to include personality among those infinite attributes. But this he refrained from doing, either because he did not recognise personality as an independent category, or else because he was in full reaction against the anthropomorphism which was then, even more than now, prevalent in religious circles. So he is led to the splendid self-abnegation of the famous utterance : He who loves God cannot seek that God should love him in return : *Qui Deum amat, conari non potest ut Deus ipsum contra amet.*[2] Yet he has no doubt that to love God is the true end and only happiness of man. " Love of the Eternal fills the soul with joy alone and is free from every sorrow : *Amor erga rem eternam et infinitam sola lætitia pascit animum ipsaque omnis tristitiæ est expers.*[3]

---

[1] *Eth.* I. Def. vi. [2] *Eth.* V. Prop. xix.
[3] *De Intellectus Emendatione*, p. 5 (*v.* V. et L.).

It will be clear what answer I should wish to give to the always open question about Spinoza. He gained the reputation of an atheist because for him God is so completely all in all that no separate God, distinct from the universe, is traceable in his writings, and because he did not find in God personality in all its functions. But he is no atheist. He is truly " the God-intoxicated man." And his love of God is so all-absorbing that he finds in the knowledge and love of God an utter satisfaction, not even desiring a love in answer. Most of us could not rise to that; and in our failure we may comfort ourselves with the thought that Spinoza's austerity is even intellectually less satisfying than the full Christian doctrine; for it presents as the ideal a human race united in devotion to a divine Reality, which expresses itself indeed in leading them inwardly to this devotion, but in itself remains eternally unmoved. It may be that apart from any historic revelation of the Divine Love, this is all that can be intellectually established; but that all-embracing circle of love which Christianity, starting with just such a revelation, sets forth as the goal of history is intellectually as well as spiritually superior. For it can fairly be argued against Spinoza that in the matter of love—to a Christian the supreme matter of all—he represents man as surpassing God. He says indeed that God loves Himself with an infinite love : *Deus se ipsum Amore intellectuali infinito amat*.[1] But in such self-love there is a quality of self-centredness, even when its object is the highest possible, that is morally inferior to the love which caused Christ to die for sinners. It is true and important that in a consequential sense God's love of Himself is a love towards men, just as their love for Him is part of His infinite love for Himself.[2] But this reflection does not make room in the conception of God for that self-giving of which the Cross is an expression.

But when this is said, the magnificence of the ideal for man remains, along with the relentless thoroughness with which the way to it is explored. And if it must be said that Spinoza was not a Christian because he did not accept a specific historic revelation, it is

---

[1] *Eth*. V. Prop. xxxv.
[2] *Ibid*., Prop. xxxvi.

only at that point that this compatriot of the
historic Christ falls short of full discipleship.
With Plato he failed to rise to belief in self-
sacrifice as a quality of the Supreme—and for
the same reason. But he believed with all
his being in the eternal wisdom of God which
has revealed itself in all things, especially in
the human mind, and most of all in Jesus
Christ : *Dico ad salutem non esse omnino
necesse, Christum secundum carnem noscere ;
sed de æterno illo filio Dei, hoc est Dei æterna
sapientia, quæ sese in omnibus rebus, et maxime
in mente humana, et omnium maxime in Christo
Jesu, manifestavit, longe aliter sentiendum.*[1]

The leading principles of Spinoza's political
philosophy, as I apprehend it, are these :

(1) Every existent thing by the law of its
nature seeks to preserve its own existence and
essence; this is the *conatus in suo esse per-
severandi.*[2] Indeed this *conatus* is itself the
" actual essence " of any particular thing.[3]
This is the fact about all things, but in the
Mind it is conscious.[4] This characteristic of
all things is the Divine Law for them. Con-

---

[1] *Epist.* LXXIII (olim xxi). [2] *Eth.* III. Prop. vi.
[3] *Ibid.*, Prop. vii. [4] *Ibid.*, Prop. ix.

sequently any distinctive Law of Duty must be consistent with this.

(2) That fundamental law applies alike to individuals and to States. Therefore when a State does what involves its own ruin, this may properly be described as Sin.[1]

(3) It also follows that true self-affirmation and absolute dependence on God are one and the same, so that in this is to be sought the foundation of virtue.[2]

(4) The *conatus* which we find in ourselves we know to be equally the law of existence for others. The aim of life, therefore, is such self-assertion as promotes similar self-assertion in others; and this it will do if it is that only true self-assertion which is in itself obedience to God.

(5) In the field of unconscious nature each thing, in being itself, takes its true place among all other things, as *e.g.* in the solar system. But when the *conatus* becomes conscious it may miss its true aim through imperfect or confused apprehension. Hence the need both for education and for the restraints imposed by society.

[1] *Tract. Pol.* IV. 4.
[2] *Eth.* IV. Prop. xviii. Schol.

(6) Thus the search for a common good, which is the foundation of society, rests on what is at once most distinctively human and most fully divine in men. Society does not arise to check the self-assertion of men in order that their selfishness may not be self-destructive, though this may be one of its functions. It actually arises out of that true self-assertion, or assertion of the true self, which is according to Reason and is obedience to God.

(7) We can now safely state the great principle that Right in either person or State is simply Power.[1] For this must be interpreted in the light of the *conatus* which alone gives meaning and direction to Power. In the pursuit of that *conatus* all that really serves it and is possible is legitimate. But what does really serve it can only be determined by reference to its true end.

---

[1] Nam certum est Naturam absolute consideratam. jus summum habere ad omnia quæ potest, hoc est, Jus Naturæ eo usque se extendere, quo usque ejus potentia se extendit. Naturæ enim potentia ipsa Dei potentia est, qui summum jus ad omnia habet; sed, quia universalis potentia totius Naturæ nihil est præter potentiam omnium individuorum simul, hinc sequitur, unum quodque individuum jus summum habere ad omnia quæ potest.—*Tract. Theol. Pol.* XVI.

(8) From all this it follows that between ruler and subjects there is an inviolable reciprocity. The ruler will only retain his authority, speaking broadly, so long as he deserves it; and the subjects owe him reverence so long as he can earn it. Thus ruler and subjects become implicated in a common effort to establish and maintain an ordered liberty.

(9) Thus liberty is the end of government; but the essence of liberty for man is to live according to Reason; and to live so is to reach after that intellectual love of God which is the love wherewith God loves Himself, and, in Himself, mankind.[1]

Several of those numbered paragraphs represent a compression of elaborate arguments or a conflation of two or three distinct passages, so that precise references cannot in all cases be given. But I trust that the outline is broadly speaking fair to Spinoza's thought.

[1] Cf. Non, inquam, finis Republicæ est homines ex rationalibus bestias vel automata facere, sed contra, ut eorum mens et corpus tuto suis functionibus fungantur, et ipsi libera Ratione utantur, et nec odio, via, vel dolo certent, nec animo iniquo invicem ferantur. Finis ergo Reipublicæ revera libertas est.—*Tract. Theol. Pol.* XX.

It has these great and marked characteristics :

(a) it closely unites politics with meta-physics;

(b) it represents the State as grounded in what is deepest in human nature and is the source of all that is best in it ;

(c) in this it presents a sharp contrast to Hobbes, who founds the State on selfishness, and whom Spinoza contradicts by refusing to regard the right or power of the State as " transferred " to it by the citizens, who are themselves deprived of what is so " trans-ferred ; "

(d) while reaching an ideal conclusion, it stands firm on the facts, and avoids all Utopianism; it reproduces the sanity of the Gospel, which bids us indeed to love God with all our being, but our neighbour as ourselves.

This survey makes it clear that Spinoza's method is very different from the deductive treatment of the subject which alone found favour in the Middle Ages.   And yet it is not inductive.   Rather it is that which Kant has taught us to call critical.   It proceeds by inquiring what is implied in beliefs or practices which either are generally accepted or can be established by demonstration. The claim of the whole scheme to our acceptance depends on its success in holding the facts of experience together in a comprehensive and coherent system. In its thoroughness, in its determination to face not only the ugly but the dreary facts, in its search for God not as outside the system but as its indwelling life, and in its ultimate idealism, it is in my judgment the most fruitful point of departure for inquiry in our own days that is afforded by classical philosophy other than that of the ancients. In what follows, I shall perpetually be responding to its stimulus, even though there is hardly one of its cardinal propositions that I could reaffirm as it stands. Anyhow, the reason for describing it at this point is because its very existence is enough to remind us that our effort to see the problem of politics in the light of our faith in God must not consist in a mere return, so far as we might be able to achieve this, to the thought of the Middle Ages. Too much has been both experienced and expressed since the year 1500 for that to be a sensible procedure. It is, indeed, a frequent experience with readers of (for example) St. Thomas Aquinas to find themselves startled by the discovery how extremely modern he is in many respects. But the materials of the problem have greatly altered, though its essence is ever the same; the elements which compose our conception of God are newly schematised; and, above all, we have acquired and inherited the historical point of view, which more than anything else is the real distinction of the modern mind.

The first effect of connecting our political thought with our faith in God is to destroy the ultimate or absolute character which has so often been attributed to the State. For that character belongs to God alone. Whatever may be the relation of the State to its own subjects, or to other States, it is certainly subordinate to the authority of God. And as other States are in the same subordination, it is involved in some relationship with them through their common subordination to Him. This is at least half of the mediæval doctrine of Divine Right. The sovereign held a divine commission; but it was not unconditional; it did not authorise the sovereign to do whatever he liked; it was a commission to uphold the divine justice. Consequently the doctrine of Divine Right was a means of setting a limit to the pretensions of rulers. If none might disobey the Lord's Anointed without sin, so long as he represented substantially the divine justice, it was the right and even the duty of citizens to depose a ruler who by tyranny and oppression transgressed the limits of his divinely given authority. And it seems at least probable that one form or another of this doctrine is the only means of keeping the sovereign within bounds. It was only the inherently absurd combination of Machiavelli's State-absolutism with a sentimental retention of Divine Right which enabled the supporters of the Stuarts to deduce from Divine Right the duty of Passive Obedience. The mediæval doctrine was something very different, as a single quotation from St. Thomas is enough to show:

"A tyrannical government is not just, because it is directed, not to the common good, but to the private good of the ruler, as the Philosopher states (*Polit.* III, *Ethic* VIII). Consequently there is no sedition in disturbing

a government of this kind, unless indeed the
tyrant's rule be disturbed so inordinately that
his subjects suffer greater harm from the consequent disturbance than from the tyrant's
government.   Indeed, it is the tyrant rather
that is guilty of sedition, since he encourages
discord and sedition among his subjects, that
he may lord over them more securely; for
this is tyranny, being conducive to the private
good of the ruler and to the injury of the
multitude." [1]

But the Middle Ages were content with the
notion of Divine Sovereignty and Justice as
the background of their theory of Divine
Right; and for this reason their sociology is
less than completely Christian.   The earthly
sovereign who is to represent and administer
the Divine Justice within his allotted sphere
must represent that quality in its Divine
associations and relationships.   It is true that
it is no function of the State to represent the
totality of the Divine Attributes; but it must
not so represent those with which it is in some
sense charged as to deny the relation in which
these stand to others.   For the Christian, God

[1] *Summa Theologiæ*, Pt. II. 2, Q. 42, A. 2.

is Love—Holy Love indeed, if the epithet is
felt to make any true addition; and His
Power and Justice are either aspects of, or
else are subordinate to, that Holy Love. This
is, of course, another way of saying that Holy
Love is the supreme good. Here we find the
answer to Plato's difficulty in reconciling the
duty and the interest of his Guardians in the
Ideal City. The State has trained their characters and intellects; they are to be asked to
repay this debt by forsaking for a time the
Vision of Good to which that training has
brought them, and governing the city in the
light of that vision. This, Plato has to admit,
is not truly good for them, except so far as
the alternative, namely, their refusal, would
be unrighteous and therefore the worst evil
that could befall them. So they will assent
because it is a just requirement that we are
making of just men—δίκαια γὰρ δὴ δικαίοις
ἐπιτάξομεν.[1] But the Idea of Good which
the Guardians are contemplating is, when
reduced to the cold terms of logic, a principle
of origination and systematisation. It is the
source both of the being of all things and of

[1] *Republic*, 520 e; cf. 540 b.

our knowledge of them : those are true divine attributes. Also it is the principle of Justice on a cosmic scale, allotting, as it were, to all other entities their spheres of existence or activity. But its own relation to all other existents is that of supremacy and nothing else; it is the highest Good that Plato could conceive; but it is not Love. If for this Idea of Good as the ruling principle of the universe we substitute the Holy Love revealed, let us say, in Christ's washing of the disciples' feet, to say nothing of Gethsemane and Calvary, the Guardians contemplating this as the highest good will recognise that in the very sacrifice asked of them is a higher good for themselves than in their continued enjoyment of the Beatific Vision. For if God is Love, sacrifice is not only a condition of entrance into Heaven, but is part of the Heavenly bliss.

In our own time such people as are exercising their minds about the influence of Christian faith on politics do not need to be reminded that God is Love, and that the State which claims, or is endued with, divine authority is therefore to exercise an authority of Love. The balance is in more danger of being upset in the other direction. It is urged in many quarters that not only is the Power of God subject to His Love, but that it is the same, and that God exercises no Power except His Love. Now it is, I think, true that for the fulfilment of His purpose in and through spiritual beings, only Love and its manifestation is either sufficient or appropriate. It is only the appeal of Love expressed in sacrifice that can call out our love in return. Yet even here there may be room for the exercise of a loving discipline using methods not naturally attributable to Love in its own nature; there is room for indignation and censure and pulverising punishment. But the spiritual sphere is not the only one. Our spiritual life is lived through animal organisms on the surface of a planet which is attached to one of a myriad stars. I see quite well how Love may be the motive prompting creation; but I do not at all see how Love, as Love and nothing else, is to be creative.[1] Love needs Power if it is to create or accomplish anything. And the difference between Love

[1] This is my difficulty with Dr. Raven's position in *The Creator Spirit*, p. 103. *See* Appendix I (p. 186).

and Power is proved in our own experience by the fact that the two do not vary together. If a man is drowning and two men try to save him, one may love him more, but if he is muscularly weak he will help less than the other who is stronger though his love is not so great. Our thought of God must be the whole Christian conception of creative and all-controlling Power acting in accordance with perfect Wisdom to the accomplishment of the purpose of Holy Love; and whatever the particular function of the State may turn out to be, we must see it against the background of that Divine Nature in its fullness.

But here another problem arises, for men pursue different methods leading to very different results in their attempt to find God in His works or to see His works as due to His activity. God is at once the Supreme Good and the Ultimate Reality. In fields of inquiry where the concept of Value has no place, the religious student merely studies the facts, confident that in so doing he is studying the works of God. In such studies we have learnt that to abandon prejudice and humbly accept the teaching of the facts is more truly

D

religious as well as more scientific than to insist in advance that the facts must conform to some preconceived hypothesis. As soon as Value comes in, the simplicity of this procedure is destroyed. Many at least will hesitate merely to review the course of human history and declare without qualification that it is the unfolding of the purpose of God. And this is not only because human wills have here played their part; theological problems are raised by the existence of creatures, such as disease germs, which from the human point of view are pests. Whatever our suggested treatment of these problems,[1] there are very few who can sincerely believe concerning human life that " Whatever is, is right." In our own time the repudiation of that belief is unusually fierce and uncompromising. In some quarters there is a tendency so to stress what I venture to call the amiability of God as to reject the thought that great historic catastrophes represent the operation of His judgment. I am not to find the activity of God either in the particular events of history

[1] I have myself suggested a theological solution of the problem of Accident in *Christus Veritas*, pp. 192–199.

or in its general course, but only in those enterprises which call forth admiration. And when I point out that in the Gospels Jesus Christ is represented as speaking of the judgment of God in terms which, however figurative, are strong almost to violence, and even as foretelling the most dreadful calamities as about to be caused by Himself, I am told that these are not to be regarded as authentic utterances, but as due in some way to the imperfectly Christianised medium of the narrators' mentality. The people who take this line usually urge us all to be scientific; but anything less scientific than this procedure cannot be conceived. In my effort to approach an apprehension of the Ultimate Reality I am to ignore a great deal of what is real and commit myself to a revelation given through the Life recorded in the Gospels; but from that record I am to omit, on no textual or other objective grounds, various passages which my advisers do not like, but which curiously harmonise with those aspects of experience which I had already been urged to ignore. That sort of thing really will not do. Let there be scientific criticism of the Gospel by all means; but let it be scientific, and not rest on personal predilections. The whole Christ of the Gospel story might be the revelation of the ruling power in a world that contains pestilences and earthquakes and interstellar spaces. The Christ of some modern presentations could only be a " Son of Man sitting on the right hand of weakness and staying away in the clouds of heaven." It is indeed supremely difficult to relate rightly to one another the two lines of inquiry prompted by the two categories of Fact and Value. The only hope lies in keeping them distinct, knowing which we are following at any particular time, and deliberately combining them, when we do so, with full knowledge and on clearly apprehended principles. I will try to set out what those principles should be according to my own apprehension, so far as they affect our present inquiry.

First then I conceive Value to be prior to Fact, in the sense that the Creative Will, which is the ground of the existence of the universe, must be conceived to act for the sake of some good; this good may be found either in the created thing itself or in some result for the attainment of which the created thing is a means or instrument. In any event, therefore, where we can say certainly that there is no good but only evil, we should refuse to see the activity of the divine Will. But on investigation it appears that nothing can thus be called evil in itself except the evil will of finite beings. Even the evil acts of evil wills are not purely evil; the conversion of will into act brings it into that system of the divine operation which is so ordered that, to the good will, all things work together for good. Of this the supreme illustration is the Crucifixion of our Lord, where the sinful act of men's evil will became the chief instrument for the conversion of that will. Coleridge was, therefore, perfectly justified when he said that there is no reason for supposing that the virtues of the Antonines have had any more to do with our present happiness (such as it is) than the vices of Nero. Our task is to unite ourselves with the divine Will, and we believe that, because our heavenly Father loves us, we can bring joy to Him by our obedience and sorrow by our self-will. But whether in union with that Will or in rebellion, we can only illustrate its supremacy; we may perhaps delay the accomplishment of the divine purpose and in so doing cause much pain and evil in the world; but even so we only afford another example of the principles of the divine omnipotence, which asserts itself against our self-will by attaching to self-will the consequences which it least desires :

> " Before man's first and after man's poor last
> God operated and will operate." [1]

Now it is quite true that such a view brings a great amount of suffering within the scope of the divine intention. But if we regard the world as primarily, in the phrase of Keats, " a vale of soul-making "; if we adopt the Christian scale of values; and if we remember the perspectives of eternity—this does not seem

---

[1] Browning, *Ferishtah's Fancies : A Camel-Driver.* Cf. the lines of Cleanthes :

> ἄγου δέ μ', ὦ Ζεῦ, καὶ σύ γ' ἡ πεπρωμένη,
> ὅποι ποθ' ὑμῖν εἰμὶ διατεταγμένος,
> ὡς ἕψομαί γ' ἄοκνος· ἢν δέ γε μὴ θέλω
> κακὸς γενόμενος, οὐδὲν ἧττον ἕψομαι.

The last line of Seneca's translation has almost become a proverb :

> " Ducunt volentem fata, nolentem trahunt."

to me to be any real objection.[1]   The Almighty Father of Christian revelation watched the dying agony of His Son without any intervention, and only afterwards converted that apparent defeat into the very stuff of overwhelming victory by the Resurrection.

Consequently, while holding fast to the faith and hope that if we could see the whole creation in its entire extent of space and time we should find it, as the Creator is said to have found it, very good, and while refusing to attribute to the Will of God the positive evil in the wills of men, we shall confidently trace the divine purpose in the general course of History, and in the immanent logic of its movement.   If we want to know God's purpose for the State, we shall not expect to find it by constructing ideal pictures out of our own heads according to our own most provisional apprehension of the values involved, but in the spirit of scientific students we shall set ourselves to discover what the State essentially is by considering what it has been and what it has done.   What anything is in the Mind of God, that it is in reality.   Where we

[1] Cf. *Christus Veritas*, pp. 197–199.

have a clear revelation, or what for sufficient reasons we take to be such, we may start with our apprehension of the Mind of God and conform our action thereto. But admittedly we have no specific revelation of God's intention for the State over and above the actual history of the State. To this, therefore, we must go.

But so we are led to the last of these general and preliminary considerations. It has been usual for those who have in any way introduced the thought of God into political philosophy to concentrate on the conception of Him as monarch of the universe. So He became the apex of the feudal triangle, with its broad basis in the common folk, its gradually narrowing hierarchy, its national apex in the King, its terrestrial apex in Pope or Emperor, and its supreme or cosmic apex in God Himself. Thus God became the fountain of all authority, as being Himself outside and above all social orders. In other words, the aspect of Deity which is prominent in the works of these political philosophers is His Transcendence. This I believe to be a mistake. I cling tenaciously to the belief in God

as transcendent, as possessing boundless resources of power and energy over and above
what appear in the normal processes of the
universe; and for purposes of conversion,
sanctification and worship I believe this to be
the more important aspect of the two. But
I do not regard the State as in any sense
supernatural—a word which, though often
misleading and always full of difficulty, I
should not hesitate to apply to the Church.
Therefore a religious political philosophy should
not attend so much to the transcendent as to
the immanent aspects of Deity. We shall not
seek the divine operation chiefly in any kind
of interventions, or in the delegation of
authority as from above, but rather in that
irresistible logic which appears in the development and history of States, attaching success
to some methods and failure to others, stability
and prosperity to some aspirations and
calamity to others. Any action of the State
which tends to destroy the State we shall
therefore regard as contrary to God's intention
for the State; though the resultant destruction is none the less due to the activity of the
divine energy.

But while these considerations will determine the general course of our inquiry, we shall still remember that we have a revelation of God, and that God is one. That immanent principle or Reason which guides all Nature, directs the course of History, and fashions the development of the State, is none other than the Eternal Word of God which was made flesh and dwelt among us, full of grace and truth. To Him therefore—as Judge and as Saviour, as announcing doom or as calling to salvation—we shall turn to check all waywardness in our speculations and to supplement all that we can learn from the historic process so far as it has yet advanced.

LECTURE II

HISTORIC THEORIES OF THE STATE

IT will assist our discussion of the place of
the State in a Christian scheme of thought if
we consider the various leading theories of the
State which have been propounded at different
times and try to estimate the degree of truth
contained in them. Neither the scope of
these Lectures nor the extent of my own
knowledge would permit an exhaustive
account, but an outline will give all that is
useful for our purpose.

There are two great types of political theory.
One takes the fact of society for granted, treats
human nature as social in essence, and holds
that some form of Government is a natural
consequence of this fact. This is the method
of Aristotle, who first plainly laid down the
proposition that Man is a social animal; [1] it
is also in reality the method of Plato, though
he conceals this to some extent by his dramatic

[1] *Politics*, I. 1252*a*, 3.

presentation of the subject. The other great type of political theory does not regard sociality as an ultimate fact of human nature, and therefore has to find the origin of society in some actual or implicit compact whereby the isolated individuals come to be members of a community to whose directions they offer their own submission and demand a like submission in their fellow-members. For the first type of theory society is a growth; for the second it is a construction.

This second type of theory has few supporters nowadays. Psychology and Anthropology have been too much for it. But it has a great history; it has exerted an immense influence; and its various forms give graphic expression to different aspects of the problem. We will therefore begin with it, and try to carry on to our own elaboration of the other type what we can learn from some of the chief exponents of the Social Contract theory.

But the exposition cannot be straightforward. If there were only one stream of development it would be a simple matter to trace it out. If there were two or more independent streams, it would be a simple matter to trace them one by one. But there are two main streams, constantly influencing each other. The exposition must be somewhat intricate because the facts are inextricably tangled.

Among the exponents of the Social Contract theory there is again a broad division, which has sometimes been obscured : the Original Contract is represented as the initiation sometimes of Society, sometimes of Government. And the fact that this distinction has not always been observed arises from the fact that many thinkers have identified Society with the State. That identification is itself, as we shall see, the one great heresy.

In Locke two contracts.

The simplest and clearest statement of the Social Contract theory is that which Plato attributes to Glauco in the Second Book of the *Republic*. It is offered as an account of the origin and nature of Society; there is in it no mention of the State or of a Sovereign. It starts, like almost all such theories, from the hypothesis of utter and absolute individualism. Men live side by side with their own desires, only concerned with the desires of others in so far as these clash with their own. To a large extent these desires are found to be incompatible; whatever one man has, ten men want; all possession, therefore, is insecure; consequently, in order that men may be selfish with some measure of satisfaction, they abandon the hope of that complete satisfaction which would arise from the successful preying upon others, and enter into a compact neither to commit nor to suffer injury—μήτε ἀδικεῖν μήτε ἀδικεῖσθαι.[1] But if anyone is so powerful that he can dispense with the protection of this compact, he will ignore it and inflict whatever injuries on others are calculated to promote his own interests as he understands them. Thus society and morality are born together, and their parents are selfishness and weakness; the really strong man will ignore them; he will not be more selfish than others, but his power enables him to give rein to his selfishness.

Before going on to more complicated forms of the Social Contract theory let us consider this simplest statement of it and note the truth which it contains. It has the great advantage of not posing as historical. Plato's

[1] 359a.

Glauco presents the Contract as one into which the citizens of civilised communities are constantly entering. This our own consciences assure us is certainly not merely false. So far as civilisation is represented by the police force it is simply true. And it is not only what we sometimes distinguish as the criminal population that provides the basis of truth for this theory. We are all quite aware that on many occasions our own conduct as good citizens depends on the existence of the law, on the means for its enforcement, and above all on the stigma attaching to those who are known to have broken any of its more serious requirements. We are all of us tacit partners to the compact that we will not do injuries in order that we may enjoy security against suffering them.

Perhaps it is best for clearness' sake to interject here a consideration which must occupy us more extensively at a later stage in the argument. The Social Contract as so far described does not impose any restriction on our real freedom, nor does it consist in any surrender of real freedom. For the repudiation of this tacit Contract would be the dissolution of society, which is not what anyone desires. The thief appropriates to himself what belongs to somebody else; but thereafter he would prefer to be secure in his enjoyment of it. The criminal does not really desire the abolition of law; the value to him of his own breach of it depends on its general continuance. Even those, therefore, who observe the law from no motive but fear of its penalties, none the less prefer its existence to any actually possible alternative. And most citizens—in fact all citizens at most times and in most respects— have other motives besides fear for observing the law, or the established custom of our civilisation; and the compact, into which we tacitly enter by accepting the conditions of civilised life, only restrains our desires so far as these are contrary to our general purpose, so that the restraints of the law are aids to true freedom, that is, to the freedom of self-control and self-direction.

But it is more important to notice that in Glauco's Social Contract there is no mention of State or Sovereign : it is not a compact of subjects with a sovereign or of subjects with one another to obey a sovereign. What it stands for is the establishment, not of a State, but of society itself. The problem under consideration was the nature of Righteousness; the inquiry was primarily ethical, and only political so far as the organised life of society is necessary to true morality. What Glauco really does establish is that even if all men were purely selfish, still society would arise as the only condition of their attaining to any satisfaction even of their selfishness. In order to draw out Socrates' answer he affirms for argument's sake that this is the actual truth about human nature and about the origin of society; but that he does not himself believe. What he establishes is not that all men actually are purely selfish by nature, but that if they were, society would still come into existence.

There was no revival of the Social Contract theory in this form as the chief principle of political philosophy until the seventeenth century; but it appears in the Middle Ages, though not in its original shape nor for its original purpose. The Church is committed to some theory of Divine Right by St. Paul. " The powers that be are ordained of God."

E

The force of the thirteenth chapter of the Epistle to the Romans is only increased when we remember that Nero was Emperor when it was written. But it was still open to discussion how this Divine Right is conferred and upon what conditions. Thus Manegold (about A.D. 1080) defended the action of Pope Gregory VII in releasing the subjects of the Emperor Henry IV from their oath of allegiance by saying that Henry had broken the agreement (*pactum*) which was the condition of his election. A similar doctrine in substance, though not in form, was held by John of Salisbury (about 1115–1180), who declares that the difference between a king and a tyrant is that the king governs according to law and himself obeys the law, while the tyrant oppresses the people by violence, and that, further, the tyrant has no rights against the people, and may be justly slain. In the turmoil of the Reformation, it was the Jesuits who made most of this theory. They strongly asserted the sovereignty of the people. This is true of Mariana (1536–1624), Suarez (1548–1617) and Bellarmine (1542–1621). In those days the question of regicide or tyrannicide was a very living one, and some leading Jesuit writers had no doubt that the tyrant might be killed; and any Protestant monarch was liable to be dubbed a tyrant. Mariana in particular defended tyrannicide, even though the tyrant was a lawful king; this brought great odium on the Jesuits after the assassination of Henri IV. But it is only fair to recall that Acquaviva, the General of the Order, formally condemned Mariana's *De Rege et Regis Institutione*, and members of the Order were forbidden to teach the lawfulness of tyrannicide. The Jesuits and Dominicans joined in a depreciation of the State for the greater exaltation of the Church.

The Reformers held a higher view of the State. Luther (1483–1546), as is well known, attributed to the local prince in practice a combination of regal and almost papal prerogatives; but it cannot be said that he had a clear political philosophy. Calvin (1509–1564), on the other hand, was far too thorough intellectually to omit so vital a department of human life from his close-knit scheme. He held that there are certain inalienable natural rights; that these are recognised by a contract;

and that there is a right of resistance against anyone who violates the natural rights, and thereby breaks the contract. But he also taught that the powers that be are ordained of God, and even under persecution steadily discountenanced rebellion. There is a noble pathos in the persistent loyalty of the French Huguenots to the worthless Valois kings. But their outlook was inevitably affected by S. Bartholomew's Day, 1572; in 1574 Beza (1519–1605) published his pamphlet justifying tyrannicide. Yet even then he was alone in the extreme form of his doctrine. Du Plessis-Mornay [1] (1548–1623) argues, in his famous *Vindiciæ contra Tyrannos*, that if the monarch be a tyrant the people may resist him; but "the people" is not the rank and file, who are distinguished as the populace; only the elect constitute the people; and no one of them may act individually; the action will only be that of the people if the elect are united under the leadership of a magistrate. The last of this series of continental Calvinists

---

[1] The attribution to him of the authorship of this most influential work seems now to be generally accepted.

whom we need mention is Althusius (1557–
1638), who first developed a federal theory of
sovereignty by conceiving the State as a corporation of corporations—a conception which
plainly involves a rather elaborate form of
contract. But with this introduction of the
subordinate associations or corporations we
hear the first intimations of a theory of the
State which is coming to its own only in our
own day.

Meanwhile in Scotland the course of events
was calling for a theory to justify the deposition
of Mary Queen of Scots. It was offered by
George Buchanan (1506–1582), who makes
legitimacy itself depend on the people's will.
Scottish history was on his side, for the
imprisonment or banishment of bad kings had
been frequent. Buchanan lays down that
there is a mutual compact between king and
people, and the king who breaks it has forfeited his right to the throne. Broadly speaking it is for the elect people to determine
whether or not he has done so. The position
of the Calvinists was not very different from
that of the Jesuits, and Buchanan's argument
has close affinities with that of Mariana; the

extremes met; there was plenty of ground for
the seventeenth-century epigram :

> " A Scot and Jesuit hand in hand,
>   First taught the world to say
>   That subjects ought to have command,
>   And monarchs to obey."

The Lutherans in Germany and the *Politiques*
in France took another view, shared with them
by the Anglican Reformers and the bulk of the
formative currents of opinion in England.   In
Germany the multiplicity of States prevented
this view from receiving full development on a
great scale.   In England it prevailed as
regards the State, but only at the cost of
altering the position of the monarch in the
State.   In France its purely political side
produced Louis XIV, and, by reaction, Robe-
spierre and Napoleon.   The supremely important writer of this school is Jean Bodin
(1530–1596).   The great contributions of the
Politiques to the progress of political thought
are two—a real doctrine of State-sovereignty,
and the principle of Religious Toleration.
They provide the rationalisation of the régime
of Henri IV.   But they have the distinction
of producing this before the facts had neces-

sitated their theory. Bodin's *République* was published in 1577, two years before the *Vindiciæ contra Tyrannos*, and Henri IV did not come to the throne till 1589. The ideas of the *Politiques* governed French policy during the period when Catharine de Medici was using the Huguenots to balance the power and presumption of the family of Guise, and when Michel de l'Hôpital was Chancellor. It was for reverting to these ideas that the miserable Henri III was assassinated.

Bodin defines the State as " an aggregation of families and their common possessions, ruled by a sovereign power and by reason." From Plato and Aristotle he had learnt to regard society as a natural unit, not resting on any contract, but finding the expression of its unity in the sovereign. He, therefore, does not properly belong to the series that we are now tracing; but it is none the less convenient to make some reference to him here. His main title to fame is that he first stated a definite doctrine of sovereignty. This he regards as a strictly unlimited power. With him Law is no longer supreme, and nothing could be further from his habit of mind than the distinction between a king and a tyrant by the test of observance of Law. "*Majestas nec majore potestate, nec legibus ullis, nec tempore definitur . . . princeps populusque in quibus majestas est rationem rerum gestarum nemini præterquam immortali Deo reddere coguntur.* Sovereignty is not limited by any greater power, nor by any laws, nor by time; the prince and the people in whom sovereignty inheres are not responsible for their actions to any save the eternal God." The sovereign, as the source of all law, is above the law. He has moral obligations to the Law of God, but these are not political obligations. Politically the sovereign—whether individual or assembly —is absolute. Bodin thus effects a clear separation between the legal and the ethical spheres within political philosophy.

Who the sovereign is, history decides. In France it was the king, whose supremacy was thus proclaimed. Bodin, quite inconsistently, held that there were some laws so organic to the sovereignty itself that even the sovereign could not alter them; such, in France, was the Salic law. Here he seems to forget his own delimitation of the legal sphere of thought and to say that the sovereign cannot do something because it would undermine the basis of his own sovereignty if he did. But this is a very minor criticism of a man who produced something so immensely fruitful as a theory of Sovereignty, and who was so far in advance of his age as to condemn slavery, to advocate religious toleration, and to inaugurate the historical method in political science alike in his use of it to determine the actual Sovereign of France and in his anticipation of Montesquieu's discussion of the influence of climatic and geographical conditions on the development of political institutions.

It is noticeable that all the names we have mentioned are those of writers who are concerned to justify certain proceedings or to provide a solution for the practical problems of their own day. This implies no censure, for even from the point of view of the most abstract science it would be true to say that the empirical *data* of political science must be the actual facts of political experience. Yet we notice some quaint results which might lead the cynic to smile. In the Middle Ages the Catholic Church taught, no less than Calvin,

that " the powers that be are ordained of God."
But of their ordination and consequent existence the Pope alone could judge with certainty. The requirement that the king, to be
a true king, must govern according to that
natural law which is the Law of God, was
pressed home in the interest of the Papal
supremacy over kings. The Calvinists argue
along exactly the same lines, so long as they
want to keep kings within bounds. Du
Plessis-Mornay bases his *Vindiciæ* on the
fundamental Calvinist tenet of God's claim to
a universal obedience. To Him alone an
absolute obedience is due. The submission
due to the king is due to him as the delegate
of God. There is a contract between God on
the one hand and king and people on the
other : besides this there is a contract between
the king on one side and the people on the
other. For this the model is supplied by the
covenant made by Jehoiada according to
2 Kings xi. 17 : " And Jehoiada made a
covenant between the Lord and the king and
the people, that they should be the Lord's
people ; between the king also and the people."
If the king violates the covenant by per-

secuting the true religion—only this time it is the Protestant religion—his subjects are thereby absolved from their allegiance. So they are if the king fails to respect and uphold the civil rights which are guaranteed by history and custom. (We must remember this when we come to Locke.) But all this was written in 1577. Seven years later, by the death of the Duke of Anjou, Henry of Navarre became heir to the throne, and forthwith the Huguenots insist, not on contracts or the right of the elect to judge when monarchs have forfeited their claim to obedience, but on legitimacy and the Salic law.

But this did not leave the theory without defenders, for it was also employed by the Catholic League, whether in the interest of the Guise or of the Spanish claims. The chief concern of these writers is to insist that a heretic could never be a lawful king. The chief object of their attack is the miserable Henri III, who is declared by Rossæus to be a tyrant of the same class as Nero and Queen Elizabeth !

The Jesuits and the Calvinists found themselves bound by sheer pressure of circumstances to set limits and conditions to the rights of the political sovereign. By so doing, however, and by the intense loyalty developed within their own religious communities, they did more for the cause of human liberty than any other schools of thought. They did not praise liberty, for they did not believe in it; but they served it greatly, for they undermined the stronghold of its chief enemy—the theory of absolute sovereignty. They were agreed also in their abandonment of the mediæval theory of a Christian society in which Church and State are different functions of one body politic; they held a doctrine of two societies over against each other, the ecclesiastical and the civil; and they limited the civil society— the State—to concern for the material basis of life, except so far as it was called upon to support the ecclesiastical society by punishing heretics and so forth. The Calvinists were more thoroughgoing in this matter than the Jesuits. On the whole they had a fiercer struggle to maintain their own religious position. And in the process these repudiators of the very thought of freedom became the champions of freedom despite themselves.

The forms of the Contract theory which we have so far considered all differ from that propounded by Glauco in the *Republic* in one vital point. For Glauco the Contract is the basis of society itself; for all these writers it is the basis of the relation between the sovereign and his subjects within a society already existing. That is always the underlying assumption; in the *Vindiciæ* it becomes explicit. Now, however, we come to a writer who revives the theory of Glauco yet makes it the basis of a doctrine of sovereignty, and that too a doctrine of sovereignty as absolute as Bodin's. In the Middle Ages and in the sixteenth century the Contract theory was an instrument for limiting the power of kings. Thomas Hobbes (1586–1679) converted it into a basis of absolutism. His system has all the merits and demerits of complete thoroughness, coherence and lucidity. Presumably the political philosophy of Omniscience has all those qualities, and possesses them as merits. But when a finite intelligence offers a perfectly neat and tidy scheme to cover all human experience, there is good ground for supposing that many of the facts have been ignored.

Hobbes begins, like Glauco, with the belief that human nature is ineradicably selfish. He makes no allowance for any altruistic motives, not even for parental or filial affection. Benevolence is " love of power and delight in the exercise of it "; compassion is " grief at the calamity of others from the imagination that the like calamity may befall themselves." In the state of nature, therefore, every man's hand is against every man. " In such condition there is no place for Industry; because the fruit thereof is uncertain; and consequently no culture of the Earth; no Navigation, nor use of the commodities that may be imported by sea; no commodious Building; no Instruments of moving and removing such things as require much force; no Knowledge of the face of the Earth; no account of Time; no Arts; no Letters; no Society; and which is worst of all, continuall feare, and danger of violent death; and the life of man is solitary, poor, nasty, brutish and short." [1] That any one of such beings may have security, everyone must be subjected to a coercive power. The

[1] *Leviathan*, Part I, chapter xiii.

method of generating this power is that men should " confer all their power and strength upon one man or one assembly of men." Thus all their wills may be " reduced into one will, and every man acknowledge himself to be the author of whatsoever is done by the ruler so constituted." [1] Thus self-assertion is made to set limits to itself while still remaining self-assertion; individualism is forced by its own logic to annihilate itself. Hobbes wished to find a remedy for the civil conflict that tormented England and France at that time—the date of the *Leviathan* is 1651; and on paper at least he did it, for he made the fountain of disorder a source of absolute rule. Consequently his form of the contract is not a contract between the citizens to respect one another's rights, as Glauco's was, nor between the citizens and a sovereign, as the mediæval contract was, but a contract between the citizens to obey the sovereign. It is therefore more than a consent or concord of the citizens; " it is a real Unitie of them all, in one and the same Person, made by Covenant of every man with every man, in such manner, as if every

[1] *Op. cit.*, Part II, chapter xvii.

man should say to every man : ' I Authorise
and give up my Right of governing my selfe
to this Man, or this Assembly of men, on this
condition, that thou give up thy Right to
him, and Authorise all his Actions in like
manner.' This done, the Multitude so united
in one Person, is called a Common-Wealth, in
Latine Civitas. This is the Generation of that
great Leviathan, or rather (to speak more
reverently) of that *Mortall God*, to which wee
owe under the *Immortall God*, our peace and
defence. . . . And he that carryeth this Person, is called Soveraigne, and said to have
Soveraigne Power; and every one besides, his
Subject." [1]

In this scheme, which I have given in the
original terms because of its immense historic
importance, two points specially concern us
here. The first is the identification of the
origin of society with the origin of Government; this was made necessary by Hobbes'
total repudiation of altruistic motives. The
other supremely important point is that while
the sovereign owes his existence to the Contract, he is not himself a party to the Contract,

[1] *Op. cit.*, Part II, chapter xvii.

and therefore cannot break it.   Nothing that
he can do by way of misgovernment or oppression can in the smallest degree invalidate his
title.

In both respects Locke (1632–1704) directly
contradicts Hobbes.   His *Treatise of Civil
Government* was published in 1690 and was
concerned to justify the Revolution of 1689.
For Locke the State of Nature is itself a social
state.   " Men living together, according to
reason, without a common superior on earth
with authority to judge between them, is
properly the state of nature." [1]   But though
it is not itself properly a state of war, as
Hobbes maintained, yet war easily arises in it.
An illustration of the state of nature is to be
found in the " rulers of independent governments " in the relations with one another.
" All men are naturally in that state and
remain so till by their own consents they make
themselves members of some politic society."
The first pact is an agreement to form some
sort of society, which must have a government, but need not have any particular
government.   This society then establishes

[1] *Civil Government*, III. § 19.

F

the government or "legislative power." But "the legislative being only a fiduciary power to act for certain ends, there remains still in the people a supreme power to remove or alter the legislature."

Thus Locke secures three results: (1) to overthrow the existing government is not to dissolve society; (2) the rights incident to any form of society, among which the right of property is for Locke conspicuous, are anterior to the establishment of government; (3) the government has a fiduciary power for the discharge of certain duties. Locke does not use the word Contract, but his position is in general very similar to that of the *Vindiciæ contra Tyrannos*. In Politics as in Epistemology he shows penetrating intuition and sound judgment, but little power of systematic thoroughness. He was trying to say the right thing, but he had not found the right vehicle for its expression. Consequently his theory is excellent in practical wisdom but poor in intellectual completeness. As T. H. Green points out, he provides on paper for an alteration of Government; but if his theory is followed rigidly, this would require such an act of the whole community as cannot in practice be brought to pass. " Having supposed the reality of one impossible event— the establishment of government by compact or by the act of a society founded on compact— he cancels this error in the result by supposing the possibility of another transaction equally impossible, viz. the collective act of a people dissolving its government." [1] Again, though Locke was genuinely interested in liberty, and his scheme is designed to make Government the guardian of liberty, his principles would have brought no hope of relief to the sectaries who were the victims of legal persecution.

If Locke had much to say that was sound, but obscured it by his way of expressing it, this is still more true of Rousseau (1712–1778), the most penetrating, the most confused, and the most pernicious of all writers on politics. He states the " problem of which the social contract is a solution " as follows : " To find a form of association which protects with the whole common force the person and property of each associate, and in virtue of which every-

[1] T. H. Green, *Principles of Political Obligation*, Works, Vol. II. p. 384.

one, while uniting himself to all, only obeys himself and remains as free as before." [1] Thus the collective body becomes the guarantor for the freedom of the individuals, and if any individual, urged on by his particular desires, comes into conflict with the general will of the collective body, he must be coerced and "forced to be free." It is only this whole body, or the general will which animates it, that can properly be called Sovereign. For the general will (*volonté générale*) is to be distinguished from the will of all (*volonté de tous*). Moreover, there is only one Contract, which constitutes the sovereign General Will. Governments are appointed in various ways, but not by any contract comparable to the first. But the General Will is to be thought of as constantly acting, though, to be sure, there is no means of telling which acts are due to it and which are not. Moreover, he has no answer, as indeed Hobbes and Locke have no answer to the question : Who are the parties to the original contract ? His answer is merely the test of residence : " to dwell on the territory is to submit to the sovereignty."

[1] *Contrat Social*, I. vi.

That may serve as a practical rule, but is devoid of any intellectual principle. The net result is a vague glorification of the Sovereignty of the People (whoever the People may turn out to be), together with a potent suggestion that the authority of Law is in principle dependent on the consent of the subjects. This being poured forth by a fervid soul had the effect of investing with a halo of romance the political expression of human selfishness. It was Rousseau who based Democracy on the assertion of Rights, and Mazzini's attempt to refound it on a basis of Duties has not yet been effectual.

Rousseau, however, was feeling after something much deeper than a theory of legal sovereignty. In our own time Dr. Maciver has drawn the distinction which Rousseau failed to draw between the Will of the State and the more fundamental Will for a State. There is a broad, deep and strong " general will " to maintain social order. This is in a certain profound sense sovereign, for it is the condition of the existence of all political power. But then it never legislates at all, and for the legal sovereign we must look elsewhere.

Rousseau's failure to draw this distinction is the fundamental source both of the confusion of his readers and of all the havoc historically associated with his name.

It is a far cry from Rousseau to Austin, but Austin is for our purposes the chief exponent of the principles of the great prophet of Utilitarianism, Jeremy Bentham (1748–1832), and all the Benthamites treated society as a construction. Bentham himself in 1822 formulated an "appeal to all nations professing Liberal opinions" with the suggestion that there should be drawn up a draft of an all-comprehensive body of law. For though he was critical of the American Declaration of Rights and deprecated the imitation of this rhetorical kind of legislation by France, yet he was ready with actual reforms for universal application. Nowhere does this abstract treatment of the body politic appear more plainly than in Austin's legal analysis of it, or his famous doctrine of sovereignty : " The notions of sovereignty and independent political society may be expressed concisely thus. If a *determinate* human superior, *not* in a habit of obedience to a like superior, receive *habitual* obedience from the *bulk* of a given society, that determinate superior is sovereign in that society, and the society (including the superior) is a society political and independent." " In order that a given society may form a society political and independent, the two distinguishing marks which I have mentioned above must unite.   The *generality* of the given society must be in a *habit* of obedience to a *determinate* and *common* superior; whilst that determinate person, or determinate body of persons, must *not* be habitually obedient to a determinate person or body.   It is the union of that positive with this negative mark which renders that certain superior sovereign or supreme, and which renders that given society (including that certain superior) a society political and independent." [1]

The chief value to us of Austin's theory of sovereignty is that it offers a *reductio ad absurdum* of this whole abstract treatment of Politics with its initial presupposition that the body politic is a construction.   Austin's theory involved, even when he formulated it,

[1] Austin, *Lectures on Jurisprudence*, Vol. I, pp. 226, 227.

the denial of the status of a political and independent society to the United States of America. Of course there is a certain obvious convenience in an arrangement which confers unfettered freedom of decision, so far as law can confer it, upon some person or body of persons; and European nations have mostly availed themselves of that convenience. But a theory which excludes from the category of political societies the Roman Republic in the ancient world and the United States of America in the modern world is self-condemned.

Austin's theory fails because he wishes to attach an absolute character to the actual political sovereign; Rousseau's fails because he wishes to regard as actual in a political sense the absolute sovereign. But one attempt or the other is inevitable if the notion of society as a construction is to be developed into a coherent theory.

The tracing of the other type of political theory will not take so long. From its very nature it called in a less degree for ingenuity of adjustments; treating political society as a natural growth, it was free to observe what actually happens and has happened, and to offer the reflections prompted by such observation as a philosophy of the State.

We have already considered the theory advanced by Glauco in Plato's *Republic*—the theory that society is a construction to which men have recourse in order to secure some satisfaction for their self-centred desires. Over against that is Socrates' picture of society arising out of the mutually supplementary capacities of different men.[1] To some extent Plato conceals his repudiation of the view that society is a construction, because he dramatically represents Socrates as constructing it; but there is all the difference in the world between a philosopher who constructs a picture of society and a philosopher who depicts citizens as constructing their own society. This latter is what Glauco does; his citizens begin as isolated individuals and resolve themselves into a society. Socrates, on the other hand, represents men as having different capacities and mutually satisfying one another's needs from the outset. The appearance of construction is due to the process of tracing out this system of mutual aid from stage to

[1] *Republic*, II.

stage. Plato, therefore, as truly as Aristotle, treats society as one function of the complex fact of human nature; as against his own Glauco he makes Socrates exhibit it as arising (*a*) spontaneously, without any transition from a pre-social stage, and (*b*) quite apart from men's selfishness.

This view, which is undoubtedly the true one, does not give rise to systems of political theory in the same way as the other, and there are few writers whom we need specially to consider. The great Roman lawyers all followed this theory, though very likely they did so unconsciously. They do not discuss how society arose, but consider the functions of its various component parts when it has arisen. This is true also of those writers already mentioned who speak of a contractual basis of Government but not of a contractual basis of society, such as Du Plessis-Mornay. But the contract remains an artificial and almost mechanical device for determining the relation of sovereign and subject, and those writers are most true to what we take to be the right method of inquiry who treat the organs of society, like society itself, as natural growths,

to be accounted for by the needs and circumstances of each State.

The first great example of this method of
inquiry after Aristotle is Bodin, who belongs
quite definitely to this series rather than the
other, though his theory of sovereignty so
greatly affected the other that we could not
omit reference to him as we traced its course.
It will be remembered that he had no Contract theory, and that he was content to
determine where lay for France the sovereignty
that he held to be indispensable, by reference
to French history. Moreover, he considered
the effects of climatic and geographical conditions on sociological development, thereby
anticipating Montesquieu.

/ Montesquieu (1689–1755) must have the
credit of effectively diverting men's attention
from the tortuous ingenuities required of
every form of Contract theory which is to bear
any relation to the facts. He had been anticipated to some extent by Bodin, and even
more profoundly by Giovanni Battista Vico /
(1658–1744). But Vico's real greatness was
unappreciated till recent times, and his historical influence was small. He dispensed with

the Contract theory, and interpreted the Law of Nature, which he believed in, according to what we should now call evolutionary principles.

Montesquieu, more than any other writer, turned the current of thought away from that realm of abstractions in which non-social individuals convert themselves into a society or generate a sovereign authority by a contract of one sort or another. Montesquieu has the distinction of making even the ideal relative : " I have often set myself to think which of all the different forms of government is the most conformable to reason, and it seems to me that the most perfect government is that which guides men in the manner most in accordance with their own natural tendencies and inclinations." [1] He regards history as a science, and believes that it is possible to trace general laws which account for the various events which seem to depend on coincidences. He regarded the influence of climate as a most potent force in determining both national character and political institutions. His ironic satire on slavery is famous, but was less

[1] *Persian Letters*, quoted by Murray, *History of Political Science*, p. 233.

influential in his own or immediately subsequent generations than the celebrated mistake about the British Constitution by which he imposed upon the United States the disastrous exclusion of Executive Ministers from Congress. But in transferring attention from abstract discussions to investigations of the concrete historical fact Montesquieu is the real pioneer, and the title of his masterpiece— *Esprit des Lois*—strikes the keynote of his method.

The chief field of Montesquieu's influence in practice was provided by the United States of America, where his ideas were propounded with a genius all his own by Alexander Hamilton; but his successor in the realm of theory was Edmund Burke (1729–1797), whose own principles were developed largely in antagonism to those elements in the teaching of Rousseau which received application in the early years of the French Revolution. As is well enough known, Burke was never more splendidly eloquent than in his denunciation of those who would take society to pieces like a machine in the belief that they could make a better machine by re-arranging the pieces. He had a vivid sense of history and its continuity. The established thing was for him a thing august, to be approached with the reverence due to the product of countless ages. This led him in some respects to an almost absurd conservatism. But it led him also to appreciate the mentality that had grown up in America, and if he was quaintly wrong about Parliamentary Reform he was nobly right about American taxation. Burke invested the State with a mystic glamour : " It is a partnership in all science, a partnership in all art; a partnership in every virtue and in all perfection. As the ends of such a partnership cannot be obtained in many generations, it becomes a partnership not only between those who are living, but between those who are living, those who are dead, and those who are to be born. Each contract of each particular State is but a clause in the great primæval contract of eternal society, linking the lower with the higher natures, connecting the visible and invisible world, according to a fixed compact sanctioned by the inviolable oath which holds all physical and all moral natures, each in their appointed place." [1]

[1] Burke, *Reflections on the Revolution in France*, Works, Vol. V, p. 184.

Here are the terms " contract " and " compact ; " but they do not represent transactions ; they stand for the perpetual recognition of an eternal mutuality and reciprocity in the order of the universe and of mankind which the Creator has established and sustains. There is no loftier assertion of the natural and divine foundation of the State than this. It is open to criticism at one important point, for it identifies the State with Society, as the context shows. And it is a view which can inspire an exaggerated conservatism. But it is a noble apprehension, and its truth within its own limits is undeniable.

Yet while Burke thus glorified the State, he cared for it as the source of that ordered liberty which is the goal of social organisation ; he condemned the revolutionary government of France no more for their lack of respect for historic continuity than for their lack of concern for individual interests. His conception of order was always rather of balance than of rigidity, and the function of Government was rather to adjust and maintain the balance than to impose a uniformity.

With the coming of the nineteenth century the currents of inquiry and speculation become so various and so intricate that our method hitherto would no longer be applicable. But broadly speaking the first part of the period was dominated by the individualistic utilitarianism of Bentham, the latter part by the mystical collectivism of the Hegelians. The transition may be traced in the writings of that most sincere and sensitive mind, John Stuart Mill (1806–1873). He began as a follower of Bentham—an individualist and hedonist utilitarian; he ended as a collectivist who had learnt to recognise the existence of many values for which hedonistic utilitarianism makes no room. But the chief contrast is between the idea of Liberty which Mill expounded in his well-known essay, and that which T. H. Green expounded in successive courses of lectures. Mill when he wrote the essay *On Liberty* in 1859 still regarded law as a restriction on liberty, though one that should only be imposed in the interests of liberty itself. Liberty in some directions is curtailed in order that wider liberty in other directions may be maintained. My liberty to walk down the road is secured by legal restriction of the liberty of whoso would desire to shoot me as I

do it. There is an obvious truth here ; but the
conceptions of both Law and Liberty in such
a view are grievously narrow. T. H. Green
(1836–1882) was insistent that Law is the
principle of Liberty in a far more positive and
direct sense; for it is not only a means by
which I restrain the liberty of others to injure
me; still more fundamentally it is the means
by which I secure my own liberty to live as a
good citizen against my own occasional desires
to act otherwise. The law that forbids murder
is not the expression of determination in one
set of people to hang another set of people if
they commit this crime; it expresses the
determination of each of us to impose restraint
upon himself if ever he feels murderous, and to
that end to vote the death penalty (or whatever
it may be) to himself if he yields to such an
impulse. Thus the murderer is hanged by
his own real will.

Bosanquet drew this logical conclusion

But the Hegelians, of whom Green is the
first and greatest representative in England,
tended to push this doctrine of the " real will "
to undue lengths; they were led to this by
their acceptance of the identification of Society
and the State. Hegel himself had bewilder-

G

ingly treated the national State as a kind of incarnation of the Absolute; all his general philosophy should have led him to find this (if anywhere in our possible experience) in the organised fellowship of mankind. His English disciples did not follow him in his virtual deification of the State, but they were not far behind. It would not be unfair to describe their political philosophy as a marriage between Rousseau's General Will and Austin's theory of Sovereignty—a union based on complete incompatibility of temper. But there is a real element of truth in both of those incongruous notions, so that the attempt to unite them was one that had to be made.

One special application of the Hegelian philosophy to politics is far from having exhausted its influence. Karl Marx (1818–1883) was not a profound or an accurate thinker. But he combined moral passion with a social philosophy which was much too simple for the facts, and therefore easily intelligible in principle, while it was expressed with tortuous ingenuity, and therefore had the appearance of an intricately balanced wisdom. It would not be appropriate here

to criticise his Political Economy; it is enough
to say that a vital part of the Marxian doctrine
is that economic development must follow a
certain course, which as a matter of fact it has
not followed.   But Marx will continue to be a
great force, because he first expressed with
insight and passion the supreme importance
of the economic factor in politics and the close
connection between economics and ethics.
Those are commonplaces to-day; but they
were novelties when Marx first insisted on
them, and he deserves in full measure the
credit due to a pioneer.

It is unfortunate that Rousseau and Marx
should have been the dominating influences in
the French Revolution at the end of the
eighteenth century and the universal economic
revolution of the nineteenth.   For it is they
who have taught the democratic movement
to take its stand on Rights.   Mazzini (1805–
1872), followed in this by Green, was never
tired of urging that the only safe foundation
for any movement of true progress was to be
found not in Rights but in Duties.   Objec-
tively there may be little difference : one
man's Duties are largely constituted by other

men's Rights. But the difference in the temper of a movement that rests on Rights will be aggressive, violent, contentious; and the temper of a movement that rests on Duties will be persuasive, public-spirited, harmonious. Mazzini was more a prophet than a philosopher, but this central theme of his prophesying was then and still is the corrective needed by most political philosophies.

Our survey is complete, or at any rate as complete as I can make it. Now we have to draw the inferences and try to combine the valuable elements in the different types of theory into a harmonious whole. First, then, we have seen the difficulties in which all theories are involved, which treat society as a construction made out of non-social material. The Social Contract theory is dialectically strongest in the form given to it by Glauco and Hobbes; but then it rests on a view of human nature which is certainly defective in so serious a degree as to be false. It contains some truth, as we saw when considering Glauco's theory; so far as society is expressed and represented by the police force, gaols, and the like, Glauco's theory is true to the social facts. Out of a similar theory Hobbes evolved a form of

absolute sovereignty; but no one ever acted
in accordance with Hobbes' theory in its
distinctive features, so that it must be pro-
nounced an ingenious fantasy. Those writers
fare little better who assume Society itself,
but try to generate the sovereign power in it
by a process of transaction; for while their
own arguments may be internally coherent,
as soon as we turn to other authors we find
precisely similar reasoning lead to diametrically
opposite results.

On the other hand, no corresponding difficulties beset those who take Society as an
actual fact of human nature, which develops
according to varying needs and opportunities.
Such writers do not ask how individuals can
form Society, nor how society can provide for
its own government. They turn to history
to trace the actual life of Society; for them,
in this connection at least, Croce's identification of History with Philosophy is a fact;
Politics becomes a positive science; and while
provision for change is, as Burke maintained,
the only method of securing stability, yet
continuity is set forth as almost the essence
of the life of Society.

Yet the labour of that other school of

thinkers was not either baseless or fruitless. Perhaps it was because the power of government so easily corrupts those who hold it; perhaps it was only that the machinery of government was not adapted with sufficient speed to function efficiently in altered circumstances; but what the whole type of " construction " theories really illustrate is a dissatisfaction with the organisation of Society in actual experience. The Sovereign was oppressive, and a means must be found of limiting his power; it is found in the notion of a contract of election or other means of appointment. That wrongly expresses an important truth—namely, that Sovereignty is an organ of Society with its own proper function, which can be transgressed. Or, again, there is civil disorder, and the Sovereign has insufficient power to check it; his hands must be strengthened; so a theory is offered which represents his subjects as guaranteeing his supremacy by the very process by which they constitute Society itself. Or, once more, it is desired to combine the security of efficient administration with a larger measure of liberty than efficiency has hitherto tolerated, so a theory is formed by

MacIver.

which men first make themselves into a society and then set up a government to serve them in certain ways. Thus we can see the meaning of the various theories of Du Plessis-Mornay, of Hobbes and of Locke in relation to our general view of Society as a natural fact, an integral part of the total fact of human nature.

The Social Contract and kindred theories point to a further truth, liable to be missed by writers of the other school. This truth is well expressed by Rousseau when he says that the problem which his theory seeks to solve is the reconciliation of obedience to law with freedom. The writers who seem to me to represent the true line of inquiry have often used an analogy almost as misleading as the Contract itself; they have spoken of Society as an Organism. Sometimes, indeed, this has been carried to ludicrous lengths. Now it is essential to the life of an organism that the several members or limbs have no independent life of their own. The analogy is perfectly appropriate when St. Paul uses it of the Church; because in so far as we are members of the Body of Christ there is in all of us only one life, which flows from Him. But this analogy of the organism must not be transferred to the civil society, to the nature of which it is quite essential that its component parts are Persons, independent in judgment and self-directing in purpose. The social order ought to be such as to express this fact, and if at any time it expresses it less than the citizens appreciate it, reform or revolution becomes inevitable.

Another aspect of this same truth is expressed by the Contract theory; the State in the last resort rests on Will and not on force. The State must have force at its disposal, for reasons that will appear more plainly as we go forward. Force, indeed, could not be the basis of anything, for it is a dead instrument which only effects what living Will uses it to effect. If at any time, as, for example, when Rousseau wrote, men who are born free feel themselves to be in chains, it is because the structure of Society, and especially its coercive machinery, does not express or correspond with the actual purposes of the citizens. The Contract theory is not even good Myth; but the Organism theory is just as false on the other side; and there are times when it is more important to stress what lies behind the myth of contract than what lies behind the myth of organism.

What all this comes to can be very simply put in the terms of the social Gospel. By common consent the two first principles in the Gospel as applied to social order are the Sanctity of Personality and the Fact of Fellowship. Society is, we find, essentially a Fellowship of Persons, and all the ramifications of social or political theory are articulations of that simple but far-reaching truth. By God's appointment we are free spirits; by His appointment also we are " members one of another." The whole problem of politics, the whole art of statesmanship, is to do full justice to both those principles without the sacrifice of either in the varying circumstances of successive ages.

And this is the arena wherein the moral and spiritual destiny of mankind is wrought out. Heroic enterprise, demonic passion, pursuit of truth and beauty, paltry ambition, humble service—all that gives significance to life, has being within this fact of Society or Community. If, then, we believe in any Divine suzerainty of the universe, we shall find here a sphere of divine activity; and to whatever has over this society an authority vindicated by society's own need of such authority, we shall not hesitate to attribute a Divine origin and a Divine Right; and of it we shall be ready with Hobbes to quote the words first spoken of Leviathan : *Non est super terram potestas quæ comparetur ei.*

LECTURE III

IT is typical of the insularity of our education in History that so few Englishmen have any conception how vitally important to all subsequent progress was the achievement of Holland in the sixteenth century. We have some knowledge of what happened in England under Elizabeth; we tend to think of the defeat of the Armada as the crowning event of the sixteenth century, by which the freedom of the northern nations was secured; and if our interest strays to the Continent of Europe at all, it is liable to find in the almost contemporaneous accession of Henri IV the event which was there decisive of the long struggle. But, as Figgis truly says: " The assured independence of the Netherlands is a greater achievement than the defeat of the Armada. . . . Henri IV sacrificed half of the principles for which he stood in order to secure success; William the Silent sacrificed only his life." [1] The Netherlands were, in influence, the dominant factor of the seventeenth century; and as in these lectures we are trying to watch the evolution of political theory and to gauge its result in the light of Christian principles, we ought not to be surprised at finding that our starting-point in each of these last lectures is best supplied by a writer who received his inspiration from the Dutch Republic.

We reached the conclusion, as a result of our historic survey, that all theories of social contract really spring from some maladjustment in the society of the moment. Society is actually rooted in human nature. It does not need to be separately explained. But when it is working badly, men are driven to seek an explanation of it which may also indicate the direction in which remedies may be found. So they analyse the State into its most obvious component parts—that is, the citizens, and seek a means by which the citizens may be regarded as not only constituting but as constructing the State in such a way as to obviate the evils which have prompted the whole inquiry. So the contract is produced

[1] *From Gerson to Grotius*, p. 218.

in many forms and to serve diametrically opposite purposes. The other and truer theory, represented by Plato and Aristotle, by Bodin and Burke, is only called forth into explicit utterance when disruptive forces threaten the fabric of society itself, as it was threatened by the Greek Sophists, by the religious wars, and by Jacobinism.

The Dutch Republic brought into the field a new type for consideration, though it is true that there was always Switzerland for men to think about. Its novelty, and the fact that its constitution was patently a construction rather than a growth, led Althusius (1557–1638) to state his theory of the state in contractual terms. But his contract is fundamentally the agreement to live in society. Here he is at one with the healthy part of Rousseau. To call this agreement a contract is misleading; but it is easy to avoid the dangers provided only that the notion is not applied as Rousseau proceeded to apply it. What is of supreme importance in Althusius is his emphatic and definite statement of the federal principle. For him the component parts of the State are not individual citizens but subordinate communities. For him the State is a *consociatio consociationum ;* its units are not individuals, but the family, the town, the province; and each of these has rights of its own anterior to the State as being part of the foundation of the State. When we remember the close connection between the Dutch Calvinists and the Puritan Pilgrim Fathers we may not unreasonably suppose that the constitution which the States of North America fashioned for their Union was not unaffected by the trains of thought which we find first clearly expressed by Althusius.

It is true that subsequent writers for many generations paid little attention to Althusius. In most countries the great problems were those of Sovereignty and Freedom. The Church was the one great corporation which claimed independence from, and even authority over, the State; and the fact that this claim was advanced alike by Jesuits and by Calvinists on the ground of the Church's divine commission prevented it from being treated as a precedent. We must therefore regard Althusius as a stimulus to further inquiry and not expect to find a succession of writers developing his germinal idea to a form that makes it applicable to modern requirements. It may even be true, as Dr. Murray says, that Althusius " is at least as important because Gierke wrote his masterpiece of mediæval learning about him, as he is for his own sake." [1] But whether it be for that reason, or for any other, he is the natural starting-point of a modern inquiry, because he, first of modern political theorists, revived the mediæval idea of the *communitas communitatum* in a form adapted to the new world which was being born in his generation.

What was once a contention advanced on behalf of the Church alone is now a plea, put forward openly or unconsciously felt, on behalf of very many associations of different types. It would be possible to give a list; but a list would have a fictitious appearance of completeness. It is best to refer only to the most conspicuous type, which is amply sufficient by itself to prove the case. There are great economic and industrial aggregations, both on the side of Capital and on the side of

[1] *The History of Political Science*, p. 159.

Trade unions etc.

Labour, which not only claim consideration by the State, but openly seek to capture and to regulate in their own interest the machinery of the State. Often these are international, overleaping the boundaries of the State's jurisdiction, so that it is impossible for them to be wholly subordinate to any one State. It is these facts which have led to the widespread revolt against the doctrine of Sovereignty as this has usually been set forth. But if the doctrines of Bodin, and Hobbes, and Burke, and Austin, and Hegel are undermined, it is not in the interest of any such position as that which was upheld in different ways by Mornay, Locke or Rousseau.

The mention of Locke in this connection reminds us of the great emphasis which he laid upon the rights of property. Here, as so often, he was correct in his estimate of the needs of his own time, but formulated his theory with so exclusive a regard to those needs that he failed to reach the real truth of the matter; and the defect of his statement made him a reactionary force in subsequent generations. The rights of property are grounded, as he partly realised, in the nature

He meant by property much more than material possessions" of Gough's Political Thought of Locke.

of Personality. The State ideally comes in, not as the guardian of property as such, but as the fosterer of the growth of Personality on which the richness of the common life depends. But as soon as this point of view is taken we realise that alongside of the rights of property there is the right to property as a necessary adjunct to a full personality. This aspect of the matter has not yet been taken up by the State.   But it will increasingly come to the fore in political life as the classes now property-less assert themselves politically. If it is a necessary duty of the State to protect existing property-holders in whatever rights it recognises, it will soon be regarded as no less a duty to provide that every citizen possesses, or can acquire, some property in which to exercise such rights.   What exactly the rights of property should be will vary according to many social conditions. But it is plain that the State, which gives sanctions to such rights, is fully entitled to determine what rights it will sanction, and is as completely at liberty to redistribute property as to protect its present owners in possession of it. But it must do this, as it should do all

H

things, on moral principles and by moral methods.

We are here on the borderland of Politics and Ethics. Before leaving it I wish to express the conviction that a Christian sociology will lay great stress on the right to property. It will not convert into a basis for legislation the sound moral principle that if a man will not work, neither should he eat, though Paulsen is perfectly justified in saying that " By the sweat of thy face thou shalt eat bread " is only a paraphrase of the eighth commandment.[1] Rather it will desire that every citizen should possess enough property to support bare life even though he does no stroke of work for it; for so his work and service will be more nearly free, and personality will have a fuller scope.

We must return, however, to the field of Politics proper and to the main course of our argument. Nearly all the theories which we surveyed in the last Lecture made one or other of two assumptions, both of which appear to be false. Either they assumed the identity of Society with the State, so that to account

[1] Paulsen, *A System of Ethics*, p. 536.

for the one was *eo ipso* to account for the
other; or else they assumed that Society
created the State by some contract of which
the terms can be inferred from the functions
which the State is expected to discharge.   At
this point the great Jesuits have the advantage
of all others, especially Suarez and Molina;
for they saw that Society is an inherent fact
of human nature, and that Sovereignty is a
necessary organ of a politically developed
Society.   Society itself does not need to be
explained in terms of non-social individuals,
nor can it be.   Again, every society has some
means of maintaining the unity of its members
in the pursuit of the aims for which it exists,
and officers (who may indeed be all the
members) for making these means effective;
when in any given community these reach the
requisite pitch of development we have Law
and the State.

The fundamental error may be thus explained : Men have been beguiled by the actual
political development of civilised mankind to
assume the territorially delimited community
not only as a necessary fact of nature, but as
the only normal social fact, and consequently to

separate in their thought the jurisdiction exercised over such communities from all other jurisdictions. It is easy to see how this occurred; it should be equally easy for any student of our times to realise that it was a complete mistake. In earlier times the lack of the means of communication made it impossible for any closely knit community or association to grow up except on a territorial basis. In our time the whole world is in a real sense one community, and there are very numerous associations of men which are quite independent of territorial connections or limitations. The territorial basis of political organisation, whenever it has been conceived as exclusive, was accidental, not essential; and theories founded upon it could not lay bare the determinant facts. These are, indeed, much simpler than most political theories would lead us to suppose, though they lend themselves less easily to tidy tabulation.

Man is essentially social. That is our starting-point. Wherever we find him, at whatever stage of development, we find some form of community. The mutual need of the sexes is the simplest and deepest instance of this; and with that goes the long period through which the human child needs parental protection and care. The Family is the root fact, and however far civilisation advances, it grows like a tree from that root.

Now even if, as is most improbable, the human race springs from a single stock, it would still be true that as the family multiplied any one of its branches would find more in common with some of the other branches than with the rest. And if there were several first " emergences " of man in the course of evolution, this would at once supply diversity of type and of interest. Anyhow, what is universally found is a consciousness of unity (broadly speaking) in each group, combined with consciousness of difference from other groups. Thus the sense of community grows from within and is strengthened from without.

At first the community is scarcely at all differentiated internally. It requires rigid adherence to its customs on the part of all its individual members. At this point such a theory as Rousseau's is the precise opposite of the fact. There has never been any problem how to generate society out of a number of free and independent individuals; the problem has always been how to find room for the freedom and independence of individuals within the actually existing social group. Primitive societies, such as those of savage tribes, allow no room for it at all, and this primitive characteristic lives on in Public Schools, Pall Mall Clubs and other sanctuaries of Good Form. To say, " It simply is not done," as a reason for not doing it, is to claim intellectual kinship with our remotest ancestors.

Very slowly, as civilisation advanced, some differentiation began to appear; and its development was marked by increasing rapidity. The Law, for example, grew more complex, and there was a need for legal specialists, who early became a community within the community. Religion in the same way claimed its specialists, and in Christendom the Church, though theoretically one with the civil society, was often, in fact, in conflict with it long before the Jesuits and the Presbyterians combined to teach the world the doctrine of the Two Societies. In the Middle Ages there was a very clear, though not often an effectual, belief in the unity of Christendom, which prevented the emergence of any theory of purely national sovereignty. But with the break-up of Christendom and the rise of nationalism the situation became defined as consisting of communities, each sovereign and each territorially delimited. That is the situation with which Grotius set himself to deal.

By that time there was abundant differentiation within these communities; there were the clergy, the lawyers, the merchants, the cloth-makers, the wool-growers and a host of other well-defined groups : I mention only those who were to be found in England. All these were within the national community; standing for that community itself there was the Crown or the State. In this primary sense the State represents and is capable of identification with the community. But it is not merely the same as the community, for it is certainly not the same as these other groups which are none the less constituent parts of the community. What then are we to say of the relation between these three terms : Community, State, Association ? If we followed the fashion of most older schools of political theory we should say that there was one universal relation between them, or at least that there was only one right relation between them. But that is just the point at which most of those earlier theories were at fault. Following Montesquieu and his school, we shall rather say that the relations have varied according to the natural conditions (climatic, geographical and so forth) and the temperaments of the several peoples. Thus Professor Unwin sharply contrasts the recent historic development of England with that of Germany : " It is worthy of remark that, whilst the main feature of British history since the seventeenth century has been the remoulding of a State by a powerful Society, the main feature of German history in the same period has been the remoulding of a Society by a powerful State." [1]

It is the comparatively recent study of Economic History which has led to the realisation of these facts. For a long while the history of a nation meant its political history, neither more nor less. Sir John Seeley

[1] *Studies in Economic History*, p. 28.

avowedly accepted this view in his celebrated aphorism : " History is past politics; politics is present history." It is mainly the questions asked by Labour as it knocks upon the doors of our Universities, that have driven the students and teachers of history to go again to their records and tell us of a wider life in the past than any which the State could possibly direct. It is as the background of such an inquiry that Unwin declared the " central and ultimate subjects of history " to be " the inward possessions and experiences of mankind—religion, art, literature, science, music, philosophy, but, above all, the ever-widening and deepening communion of human minds and souls with each other." These, he says, " embody not only the main outcome of history, but also its main creative factors." [1]

Like most new enterprises of research, Economic History has had a damaging effect on many reputations. Thus there has been a beautiful legend of Edward III, who earned the title " Father of English Commerce " by establishing the cloth industry in England. But it appears that the facts do not corre-

[1] *Studies in Economic History*, pp. 3 and 14.

spond. "Edward III did not establish the cloth manufacture. He found it expanding and taxed it." [1] I mention this legend because it is illustrative of the main argument. The facts exhibit a sharp distinction between the living movement of Society and the action of the State. Under the influence of an *a priori* theory which identifies them, men have attributed to the State what in fact Society was achieving not only without, but even despite, the action of the State.

Professor Unwin goes so far as to follow this into regions where the decisive character of State action is usually taken for granted. He finds no evidence that the future history of North America was really determined by Chatham's policy and Wolfe's victory. " The expansion of England in the seventeenth century," he writes, " was an expansion of society and not of the State. Society expanded to escape from the pressure of the State; and when the State, in consequence of the duel with France and the conquest of Canada, attempted to follow up the expanding society and to re-establish its pressure, a federation

[1] *Studies in Economic History*, p. 7.

of new States arose to resist the realisation of an empire which had so far existed merely for the purposes of rhetoric. . . . Nor is there any reason to think that, if Montcalm had defeated Wolfe at Quebec, the swamps of the Mississippi and the prairies of Manitoba would have been reclaimed by French pioneers." [1]

Clearly it is impossible to say with any approximation to assurance how much or how little military victories may have had to do with " the expansion of England." But at least it is wholesome to balance Sir John Seeley's well-known presentation of the matter with such an utterance as has just been quoted. It is not relevant here to adjudicate between Seeley and Unwin. It is enough for our present purposes that such a view as that of Professor Unwin is even possible. For that alone is enough to show that the identity of Society and the State cannot be taken for granted.

But if the State is not Society organised as a unit, what is its essential nature ? We will once more quote Professor Unwin. " I mean

[1] *Studies in Economic History*, p. 341.

by the State that one of our social cohesions
which has drawn to itself the exercise of final
authority, and which can support that authority
if need be with the sanction of physical force.
And I mean by Society all the rest of our
social cohesions—family, trade union, church,
and the rest. Now human progress and
human liberty have depended and continue to
depend on the multiplication of our social
cohesions, and on the withdrawal of final
authority and of the sanction of force from
all our social cohesions except one—the State.
Primitive man was restricted to a single
cohesion, which controlled him with supreme
authority. Life was impossible outside his
tribe. Freedom was impossible within it.
The great array of differentiated social cohesions, which represent in their totality the
free society of modern civilisation, and from
which the authority and force embodied in
the State have withdrawn themselves, furnish
the individual with that great variety of
choice which constitutes real freedom. When
a man marries a wife, chooses a trade, joins a
church or a political party, he limits in each
case his ability in the abstract by an act of

Societies voluntary
State compulsory.

social cohesion. But a man of character can, we know, extract more freedom from such a set of relationships than he could achieve by remaining a bachelor, being an independent gentleman and belonging to no political organisations. The new social cohesion he has entered—his wife's kindred, his church, his party—impose, no doubt, new obligations, but they also furnish new scope for his personality. They are not a mere instrument of social pressure. He can react through them upon Society, and this reaction of a strong and clear will upon Society is freedom. But this is only possible on condition that he freely selects his social cohesions and that no one of them except the State has final authority over him." [1]

I have quoted that passage in full because in it Professor Unwin, on the basis of his great knowledge, gives summary expression to the view which I desire to commend. The main points are these : (1) Society is more than the State, and has a life which is largely independent of the State; (2) social progress largely consists of the expression and develop-

[1] *Studies in Economic History*, p. 459.

ment of that independence; (3) the State is distinguished from other " social cohesions " by the fact that it alone is entitled to use force in order to secure obedience to its commands.

This is true so far as it goes. But to make force the differentia of the State would be disastrous, and the term " social cohesion " requires explication. To the avoidance of the error which makes force the distinguishing features of the State we are greatly assisted by the two admirable books of Professor R. M. MacIver—*Community* and *The Modern State*. In the first of these he reaches by a rather different route the main conclusion cited from Professor Unwin—that Community or Society is more than the State, and that human history is therefore more than the history of politics; in the same book he establishes the important principle that individuality and sociality, far from being mutually antipathetic, develop together. In *The Modern State* he takes up the inquiry, What is the place and function of the State within the community? He first points out that even when the State has claimed control over every sphere of life, it has never been able to exercise it; there have always been areas of life, and of social life, which it could not direct. For this reason he calls it an Association, as distinct from Community or Institution. Here, I think, he is mistaken; his argument to establish this result follows the method of elimination : the State is not either Community or Institution; therefore it must be an Association. But the catalogue of possibilities is, I think, not exhaustive; and Professor MacIver seems to have fallen into the very common error, denounced by himself, of thinking it necessary to conceive society and the State by means of analogies.[1] It is not an organism, it is not a contractual construction; equally, I should maintain, it is not an association. To that we shall return; but the fact from which this wrong conclusion is derived is a most important fact. The State does not and cannot control the whole of social life.

At first sight it is distinguished by its admitted right to employ force. Whence is this right derived ? It cannot be from the

---

[1] *Community*, p. 89. *The Modern State*, pp. 447 ff.

mere fact of a claim to sovereignty. " The tyrant who subdues men to his irresponsible will is no more exercising the function of political government than the bullying schoolboy who by his brute force cows his companions into obedience." [1] The right of the State to employ force is derived from the fact that it alone acts for a community of such a kind that actual membership of it cannot be repudiated. There are other forms of membership which are involuntary, such as membership of the family. Nothing can abolish that membership as an historical fact; none the less, all its obligations may be repudiated. But the obligations of membership in the national community cannot be repudiated. The course of history has led to the formation of these great geographical unities, and has so far covered the world's surface with them that, broadly speaking, if I leave the confines of one I must enter the confines of another. There is a *de facto* universality about the claims of such a community which makes the Law enacted by its accredited agents quite different from the rules of membership in

[1] *The Modern State*, p. 16.

any ordinary association. If I disagree with my political party I can leave it. If I dislike the rules of my club I can resign my membership. But if I am opposed to the requirements of the State, made in the name of the national community, I can only put myself outside their scope either by transferring myself to the territory of another State or by forgoing the advantages of civilisation altogether. Thus the State has a universal authority over its members such as is not elsewhere to be found. The force with which the State is entrusted is the means of making actual and effective this universality of Law.[1] And force is confined to the State in order that its exercise may always be in the service of Law.[2]

Both this universality, and the force by which it is expressed and guaranteed, at once set limits to the appropriate spheres of its action. Because of its universality, Law can only deal with general situations; it may provide, also as a general principle, for the

[1] Cf. *The Modern State*, p. 230. " It is the universality of the State, within its range, which makes force a necessity." [2] *Ibid.*, p. 151.

I

exercise of discretion in its own application, as in the prerogative of mercy; but it cannot itself take account of individual considerations. Because its instrument is force, it cannot control opinion or aspiration, which tend to be repelled rather than directed by the application to them of any form of coercion. Consequently " the State serves best when it provides the liberty and order on which other associations can build, and by which they seek more intimate or more particular ends." [1]

The distinguishing mark of the State, then, is not its possession of force, but its self-expression through Law, which employs force as the guarantee of that universality which is its essential nature. Hence those philosophers, from John of Salisbury to Mornay and Locke, who distinguished kingship from tyranny by its conformity to Law were in principle perfectly right. The Majesty of Law is the foundation of a secure and progressive civilisation.

But this Majesty is a historic result, not an aboriginal endowment. It has " emerged "

[1] Cf. *The Modern State*, p. 20.

(as the biologists of the moment like to say) out of the rigidity of primitive custom. And here we find the distinction between the State and an Association. As social life differentiated itself various associations grew up within society; but the State did not so grow up; it is the organ of the community itself over against its own members or associations. It comes into independent existence through the formation of specialised associations within the Community; as these are formed for the service of special interests the State is found standing as the guardian of Community itself. It is the residuary legatee of the primitive social unity. This was inevitably geographically determined, because, as has been pointed out, apart from modern means of communication there could be no intercourse sufficient to generate very close ties of community except within a limited area. In the Middle Ages the primitive sense of undifferentiated community still prevailed in men's minds, but the influence of the Church extended this to cover Christendom; in that period, which was far more effectively international than the sixteenth, seventeenth, eighteenth and nineteenth centuries, the national community was still in process of realising itself under the shadow of the universal Christian society. General progress was leading to sharper differentiations, and in the Renaissance both Art and Politics broke loose. Since then the process of emancipation has gone forward apace, and the modern Church (to use again the phrase employed before) is historically the residuary legatee of the mediæval and Catholic idea. Many believe, and still more hope, that a redintegration is already commenced which may reconstitute the unity of human life, not under the coercive control of a Church-State, but under the permeating influence of Religion using the Church as its special but by no means its only organ.

However that may be, the first result of the emancipation of Politics from a theoretical religious control was the rise of national sovereignty as the one means of securing the liberty and order which alone make social life possible. Like most reactions, the movement in this direction was exaggerated and went some way towards a return to the rigidity of the primitive community. It cannot be too strongly asserted that, however necessary it may have been as a phase of progress or rather as a pre-condition of further progress, the Renaissance in its political aspect was rather retrograde than progressive. It went back in thought to that first phase of real civilisation, the City-State, which was so small that State and Community could be identified without much loss. The fact that this form of social experience provided the data for the first two great philosophers, Plato and Aristotle, has led to the perpetuation even into our own time of that disastrous identification. The historical method is the great distinction of the modern mind, and it is only of recent years that men have learnt to read the great philosophers in their historical context, so as to see where their authority is applicable to our problems and where it is not. The Renaissance was negatively a repudiation of the sovereignty of the Church over practice and of Theology over thought; positively it was a return to the pagan ideals of Greece and Rome. Its first green vigorous shoots appear in Machiavelli; its flower is Louis XIV; its fruit is the French Revolution, both in the idealism of 1789 and in the Terror of 1793–94.

In England the process went forward more quickly; our Renaissance had its flowering time under Elizabeth; but from reaping its bitterest fruits we were saved (under the mercy of Heaven) by the stupidity of the first two and the last of the Stuarts. The Revolution of 1689 introduced a mixed constitution with no very effective sovereignty discoverable in it, and we entered on a period of social advance and political stagnation till Society was strong enough to remodel the State—a process which began to be effective in 1832 and is not yet finished.

It is only in the writings of some philosophers and the semi-conscious theories of ordinary citizens that the State has preserved its universal sovereignty. Men still talk about its omni-competence; but its total incompetence to settle the affairs of the coal industry is the chief feature of English political life in the last two years. This theory of omnicompetence has so far outlived any correspondence with the actual facts that it is become partly ludicrous and partly perilous;

for there are those who wish to act upon it, and to do so may easily involve the destruction both of the State and of the community which it safeguards.

The Institution which has shown most power of adaptability in our own social and political system is the Monarchy; if I rightly interpret the popular sentiment of our day, it does not regard the King as chiefly the head of the State, but rather as the impersonation of the Community—a greater thing. When the King opens Parliament, we see the Community, in his person, calling on its servant, the State, to discharge its functions.

MacIver admirably grades the terms which have played so great a part in political theory. First, there is the General Will. But "this is not so much the will *of* the State as the will *for* the State, the will to maintain it." [1] This is the ground of our obedience to laws of which, in themselves, we disapprove; it is not itself a fount of legislation; it never overtly acts at all. But it is the source and ultimate sanction of all legislation. Next there is the Will of the People, so far as this

[1] *The Modern State*, p. 11.

expresses itself; in a democracy its instrument is the vote; under other constitutions it has to employ other forms of pressure, with the threat of revolution in the background; this MacIver calls the Ultimate Sovereign, because it ultimately determines the general policy of the State. Thirdly, there is the Government, which, established or tolerated by this Ultimate Sovereign, acts as Legislative Sovereign, and translates general policy into the particular enactments by which it is carried out.[1]

These three elements are always present. What the precise relations between them are or ought to be will depend on the actual historic development of the community. But it may be reasonably claimed that, where other conditions do not hinder, elective democracy is the system which most fully corresponds to the actual political fact; what is vital, however, is that the Ultimate Sovereign should have some means of changing the Legislative Sovereign without breaking up the machinery of the State. This in England is provided by a General Election at fixed

[1] *The Modern State*, pp. 12, 13.

intervals. As long as the Ultimate Sovereign can thus control the Legislative Sovereign, there is little danger that the General Will of the individual persons concerned, to live as a community and submit to any restrictions necessary to that end, will be impaired. And this is the vital matter.

The State and the nation grow together. It is hard to give an account of either which does not refer to the other. " Nationality," says MacIver, " is the sense of community which, under the historical conditions of a particular social epoch, has possessed, or still seeks, expression through the unity of a State." [1] Nationalism has been the great feature of the last three centuries; consequently State absolutism became the dominant political philosophy. Now life is becoming increasingly international; as the associations and communities in which men are conscious of membership become increasingly independent of national frontiers, though the national community itself remains, the State becomes less absolute and feels its way towards determinate relations with other States, first

[1] *The Modern State*, p. 124.

by international law, and now by a League of Nations. This aspect of the question will chiefly occupy us in the next Lecture. But simultaneously within the nation there is a growth of associational life wholly beyond the power of the State to control. More and more of the State's former area of sovereignty is withdrawn from it. The Modern State is the residuary legatee of the Renaissance Leviathan, as every civilised State is of the primitive social unity.

As such the State is as necessary as ever it was to human welfare. The more complex our associational life becomes, the more important is that universal Law which the State upholds. Only if the general fabric is firm and reliable is there freedom for spiritual, intellectual or commercial enterprise. Here we come once more upon the fundamental characteristic of Law. It is desirable that it should be just; it is essential that it should be stable. An all-wise despot could deal with individuals more justly than the Law, with its neglect of individual considerations, can pretend to do. Yet the reign of Law is better than such a despotism. For we, who are not all-wise, would not be able to predict the actions of the all-wise despot; to us they would seem capricious; we should have nothing to count on; we should not be free to plan and to choose. A bad law firmly administered gives a foundation on which men may build at their will; a good law loosely administered supplies no such foundation. It is important that the laws should be as good as we can make them, and the process of improving them by no means impairs their value. But that value entirely depends on their having the quality of Law, which is absolute universality. This will involve a certain crudeness and even callousness in the treatment of many individuals; yet for those individuals themselves, as for all other citizens, the quality that involves this crudeness is the indispensable condition of much that is most delicately intimate in human life.

We may now attempt something approaching a definition of the State; we shall adopt with slight modifications that of MacIver, and say that *the State is a necessary organ of the national community, maintaining through Law as promulgated by a government endowed to this end with coercive power the universal external conditions of social order.*[1]

The State is an organ of community; it has a derived existence and a conditional authority. It is not, therefore, an ultimate object of loyalty. The ultimate object of political loyalty is the national community. Normally the State is necessary to the community; therefore normally there is a loyalty due to the State. But the State may be so ill-administered, or have fallen into so grave a maladjustment to social needs that, failing the means to reform it, there may arise a duty to the community to destroy the existing State that another may be set up instead of it. Many will hold that the Revolution which overthrew the Tsarist State in Russia was justified on these grounds, however completely they condemn the *régime* which was shortly to take its place.

Moreover, though man is essentially social, he is not merely social; still less is he merely political. He is also a seeker for knowledge, a creator and lover of beauty, a worshipper of God. If the State forbids him to pursue

[1] Cf. *The Modern State*, p. 22.

knowledge or prescribes the manner of his pursuit of it—if, for example, it forbids him to seek biological truth, or orders him to seek it only in the Bible—it is going beyond its true function; to refuse obedience in such a case is not only permissible, but is a duty both to truth and to the community. Such action on the part of the State is destructive of a whole sphere of values which the community should become increasingly able to enjoy. It is in the same way a duty to resist any effort by the State to control æsthetic creation and appreciation. But most of all is the authority of the State out of place in determining how men shall worship God. For a long time it was supposed that religious diversity must be incompatible with political unity. It has long ago become clear that, if this was ever true, it is true no longer. The State is, no doubt, perfectly at liberty to say to a Church what are the conditions on which the relations of Church and State called Establishment may exist or continue; but it exceeds its proper province if it uses the machinery of Establishment to impose or to prohibit any forms of worship. For the State is here challenging claims more august than its own, or even than those of the national community, and that too in a region where even more than elsewhere its weapon of force is futile. It is sometimes asked whether the State is not the most important of all the organs of man's common life; but there is an ambiguity in the word "important." The State is the most indispensable—more indispensable even than the Church. It is the pre-condition of the maintenance of all common or social life. But it is only the pre-condition. The higher values of that life are established upon the foundations which it provides, but are themselves beyond its cognisance. If the State in its general co-ordination of the common life seriously restricts in freedom of action one of the associations specially concerned with any of these higher values, that association may be bound *in duty to the community* to resist the State; for in such a case the State is impoverishing the common life which it exists to preserve and to foster.

It is such considerations as these which prove the great importance of political theory.

Because the State acts through Law, and the essential quality of Law is universality, there is a tendency in those who administer the State to claim a universal jurisdiction. This is right if what is meant is a jurisdiction over those functions of all human activities which are properly amenable to Law as safeguarding the universal external conditions of well-being. The State has a perfect right, and a bounden duty, to exercise jurisdiction over the Church (or the Royal Society or any other corporation whatsoever) as a holder of property. But it exceeds its province if it tells the clergy what they shall preach or the men of science what they shall discover. It is universal in that it is concerned with all life in certain respects; but it is not universal if that term is understood to mean that it is concerned with all life in all respects. A false or confused political theory may easily lead statesmen to act in a way that impairs the fullness of life in the community and, by reaction, imperils the very existence of the State.

Again, it is perfectly true that the State, as fountain and guarantor of Law, has no political superior. No legal limits can be set to its authority. But this must not be construed as endowing the State with positive omni-competence; if that is done, the theory conflicts with the reality in most dangerous ways. The State cannot compel a man to murder his mother. No one can prevent it from ordering him to do so; but if it does so order it will discover the limitation of its power; for not only will the man disobey, but if the State tries to punish him for disobedience, it will raise its own citizens in rebellion against it, and find that, though it has no legal superior, it can only exist so long as the community desires that it should or acquiesces in its doing so.

The illustration just given is, no doubt, an absurd one, though it suffices to establish the principle. But it is not so very remote from a situation into which modern nations may drift. The great problem of our day is the relation of the State to the economic groups which exist within it, but also overlap its boundaries. There are great aggregations of Capital and of Labour; both are to a considerable extent international. The maintenance of peaceful relations between them is essential to the welfare of the Community. The State is fully entitled to take any steps that are genuinely within its power for the maintenance and permanence of those peaceful relations. But just what steps are within its power? To coerce Capital may be to drive it abroad and so, by increasing industrial depression, to destroy what the coercive action was designed to preserve. On the other side, to put forth the force of the State against Labour on strike may be to call on the working man who is a soldier to shoot his fellow working man, who may also be his father or his brother; and the soldier may refuse to do it.

Such problems do not arise when society is in perfect health; but our society is not in perfect health. The adjustment of the social and economic order and of the political system has not kept pace with the development of social life. Consequently there is grave discontent with the State as an organ of the community, sometimes amounting to a spirit of revolt against it. All of this came to a head in the so-called General Strike of 1926, // and it will be instructive to see how that

K

experience and our theory of the State bear upon one another.

A vast body of opinion in the section of society called Labour believed (rightly or wrongly) that there was then imminent a general attempt to reduce wages, and that the notices posted by the mine-owners announcing serious reduction of the miners' wages was the first action in pursuit of this policy. This was an attack on their own amenities; but the determination to resist was not purely selfish; it was partly based on the conviction that the anticipated reduction would be bad for the whole community of which Labour is so great a part. To the forces of Labour it did not appear that they were holding the community to ransom, but that they were preserving the community from depredations threatened by the capitalist classes. There were certainly many who joined in the strike, after the failure to secure by negotiation the withdrawal of the notices at the pits, out of loyalty to the community and in the interest of its welfare as they understood it. Such persons cannot be justly called revolutionaries. On the other hand, their action was fraught with peril to the

State, and if they were not revolutionary, their action was. Consequently the spokesmen of the State, that is, the Government, were bound to refuse to negotiate until the revolutionary menace was withdrawn, even though they knew that by most of the strikers no revolution was intended. At the same time the State, or the Government which wields its power for the time being, is bound to recognise in such an event a symptom of serious maladjustments either in the community or between the community and itself or both. The strikers were just as much entitled as the Government to form an opinion of what the welfare of the State required and to act on it. It may be that in a democracy it is never right to resort to such an expedient as the General Strike, because a General Election is never far away; but if so, it is because the cost is always greater than it is necessary or worth while to pay. The method is to be condemned because it is bound to do more harm than good, not because it is inherently wicked or disloyal.

The most significant feature of the actual General Strike of 1926 was the law-abiding conduct of both strikers and others, and the effect upon the strikers of the declaration that their action was illegal. The General Will— the will for a State—was thereby proved to be both vigorous and loyal. But the episode itself was none the less evidence that the General Will has been subjected to severe tension, beyond what it is desirable to risk.

Do our principles give any indication of the direction in which a remedy for this state of affairs may be sought? On the one side is the demand that the State should do nothing; this comes from those who suffer least from the present situation. On the other side is the demand that the State should assume complete control of the industry; this comes from those who suffer most from the present situation. It would not be fair to say that either party wishes to exploit the State in its own interest; but it is quite fair to say that each party is trying to exploit the State in the interest of a conception of the general welfare which is based on a one-sided experience.

In distinction from both these lines of policy our principles would suggest some method of devolution of authority upon bodies based on voluntary associations. The first necessity is to give full recognition to any association which has shown that it possesses real power of influencing the situation. That step has been taken so far as (for example) the Government has had direct dealing with the Miners' Federation. The principle is that as soon as any group possesses actual power it must be treated as responsible. Then, if it be possible, let there be formal conferences between the different associations concerned in any dispute or liable to be brought into dispute; if these conferences reach results requiring legislation, let there be facilities for such legislation, provided that the State watches the interest of the community generally in passing such legislation.

Hitherto the method has been to hold an inquiry by means of a Royal Commission; but the responsibility for initiating legislation has lain with the Government. This is bad, because it tends to set each of the two parties to the dispute endeavouring to win the Government to its own one-sided view. Our principles suggest that a conference of the two parties be summoned and endowed with legislative power, subject to the veto of Parliament as representing the community. It is not suggested that every industry should have a private legislature of its own, but that Industry should have its own Industrial Parliament, based, largely at least, on the voluntary associations which have grown up and will still grow up in Industry; this Industrial Parliament should be possessed of legislative power in its own department subject to the veto of the national or imperial Parliament. Such a system could not be inaugurated at once; there would be many intermediate steps to take. But the sound principle, if our whole contention is right, is to throw upon the conflicting voluntary associations the legal responsibility for maintaining their own peace. The State for its part should be glad to hand over to others all responsibilities except that for the community itself.

The Church has in England set an example that might well be followed. Being unable, because of the pressure of other claims on Parliament, to obtain legal sanction for reforms that were needed, the Church constituted an

Assembly by which it was willing that legislation affecting it should be framed, and asked Parliament to agree that legislation so framed should become operative after a single favourable vote in each House of Parliament. To this, subject to certain safeguards, Parliament assented when it passed the Church of England Assembly (Powers) Act in 1919. The resultant constitution leaves subject to Parliamentary review certain matters that ought ideally to be finally settled by the Church alone; but we are not now concerned with the ecclesiastical question.[1] Our present concern is with the constitutional principle followed, which seems to be full of promise.

We have already outlined its possible application to the field of Industry. An equally obvious field for its application is Education. The State cannot educate. It can only supply educational facilities and compel attendance. These functions are theoretically discharged through the Board of Education. There is a Board of Education, but if it ever meets no one hears of the fact. It consists of a few specified Cabinet Ministers.

[1] See Appendix II. (p. 190).

In practice the work is done by a staff of Civil servants under the presidency of the Minister for Education. This works tolerably well, but is none the less thoroughly unwholesome. The Codes issued by the Board are bureaucratic productions, and teachers feel no loyalty to them though they have to obey them. Our principles suggest the conversion of the Board of Education into an educational Parliament, representing the Universities, the Local Education Authorities (through their own Associations), the National Union of Teachers, the Teachers' Registration Council, the chief religious Denominations, and (by Parliamentary appointment) the general public. To such a body might be given powers of legislating concerning education subject in one way or another to Parliamentary veto. This body would employ the Inspectors and allocate the money voted by Parliament for its distribution. My own hope would be that it would prescribe very little in the way of curriculum, leaving teachers free to experiment as they wished. In this and in other departments the State would learn to endow activities the control of which was not in its own hands but in the hands of bodies representing the voluntary associations concerned.

These various bodies would not become part of the State. They would be means by which the State recognised and entrusted with responsibility in their own spheres the voluntary associations. We could find precedents for such action in the history of the Universities, the Inns of Court, and the General Medical Council. Their decisions would only acquire the force of law through the assent of Parliament and the Crown. The State would retain its legal supremacy and its exclusive right to make actual law; but it would devolve the framing of law on voluntary bodies and would thus make these responsible not only for the possibly selfish interest of their own members, but also for the general welfare, while setting itself increasingly free to discharge its one unalienable function of safeguarding the community as a whole.

Such a line of development in general, however much modified in detail, seems to be demanded by the immanent logic of the history of the State. The great principle is that the Constitution should be constantly adapted so as to secure that the political system corresponds with the moral facts. One great moral truth is that power involves responsibility. Therefore, wherever there is power, responsibility should be formally bestowed; then even associations which have been formed for selfish purposes, if they obtain actual power, will be converted into agencies of service.

It is hardly necessary to ask how such a proposal squares with Christian principle. If we take the four " secondary principles " mentioned in the first Lecture,[1] it appears to be in full harmony with three, while the fourth, the Power of Sacrifice, lies beyond the sphere of political organisation. Such a scheme as has been outlined gives the fullest possible scope to Personality; for this reveals itself largely in special affinities and in the associations which embody these. To increase the scope of these associations is thus a potent method of fostering the growth of Personality. The same policy plainly recognises and rests on the Fact of Fellowship, for fellowship is

[1] See above, p. 5.

chiefly realised through those same affinities and associations. But above all it stresses the Duty of Service; for it takes associations originally self-centred and sometimes even selfish, and bids them take counsel for the common good. There is danger here, as there was danger when the elder Pitt recruited the Highlanders lately in rebellion for his Canadian and other armies; but by taking that risk he pacified Scotland.[1]

This seems to be the great principle alike of Christianity and of statesmanship : wherever you see Power, call on it for service. But it must be real service, voluntarily rendered, not mere labour grudgingly given. So there will be a risk to be taken. But to avoid that risk is to accept the certainty of warring factions, with the State as no more than referee of their fight. If the State calls them into its own service, not only by verbal appeals but by giving them real opportunity and responsibility for taking that opportunity, it may convert them into comrades, while itself, instead of watching a fight, can do its

[1] Cf. Basil Williams, *The Life of William Pitt, Earl of Chatham*, Vol. I. p. 294.

proper work of harmonising in the one life of the community the services of its various constituent groups.

Moreover, such a system recognises that Man is more than the citizen of a State. It not only leaves him free, but openly encourages his exercise of freedom, to make his own associations according to the gifts that God has given to him and to his neighbours. The State with its Law supplies the firm foundation on which man can build the spiritual edifice of a corporate life transcending earthly limitations. The State is still necessary to him while he lives on earth, but it suffers nothing from his claim to possess a higher citizenship than it has to offer. The humblest child of God has a rank above that of earthly emperors. The State as we have conceived it will help him to live worthily of his high destiny, and will fulfil itself in supplying the external conditions which make possible a spiritual development for ever beyond its ken.

LECTURE IV

THE mediæval world inherited from the Roman Empire and from the Stoics a belief in the unity of civilisation; this received both consecration and actuality through the Catholic Church in the form of the unity of Christendom. The great disputes of the Middle Ages did not arise concerning the relation of national States to Christendom, but arose from different doctrines about the focus of unity in a Christendom admitted to be one. Was the Pope alone the head of this society, or did Pope and Emperor hold a joint authority under God? There is no doubt that the Imperialists have on their side the greatest names, for though S. Thomas Aquinas was distinctly a Papalist, this is not so constitutive an element of his whole political doctrine as Imperialism is for Dante (1265–1321), or the idea of the secular State and of a General Council as superior to

141

the Pope for that astonishingly modern personage, Marsiglio of Padua (c. 1278–1343). But perhaps more representative than such men of the first rank in genius is the effort of the brilliant but less solidly grounded Pierre du Bois (c. 1255–1312) to claim for France the leadership of Europe which the Empire seemed incapable of sustaining. That he makes this claim for his own king is a sign that that national spirit is moving, which, a century after his death, Joan of Arc was to call into vigorous and most effective vitality. But the fact that Pierre wished to secure the unity of Christendom by placing the Imperial crown upon the head of the king of France shows that nationalism had not yet destroyed the sense of an actual unity existing in the world. Louis XIV and Napoleon followed other methods.

It is possible that if the Conciliar Movement had been started earlier it might have saved Christendom. As it was, it certainly came too late. The Council of Constance met in 1414. Henry V was on the throne of England, and this country's part in a great movement for world-unity was to indulge in the worst of all our fits of that disease which our generation calls Prussianism, because Prussia was the last to have it. In reaction Joan of Arc evoked the national spirit of France. The Councils were all too late. It is true, of course, that they were not summoned to create international unity; but they were summoned as international bodies to reform the Church which in theory, and to some extent in fact, held all the nations together. Their failure to reform the Church from within necessitated the great cleavage of the Reformation, and out of the ruins of the single Christian society arose the omnipotent national State. The Reformation may or may not have given us pure religion for individuals; it certainly left us with a very practical form of Cæsar-worship in our politics.

Whether after this there has been any real opportunity of restoring the fellowship of nations may be doubted. It is apparently uncertain whether or not we can take very seriously the " great design " of Sully, or his attribution of such a scheme to Henri IV. Anyhow it is profoundly interesting that such a design should have been even formulated at the very beginning of the seventeenth century; for it combines both the notions which dominate international politics in our own day, the Balance of Power and Federation. Europe was to be divided into a number of equal Powers; these were to form a Christian Commonwealth, with rules of arbitration for the prevention of war, with universal freedom of trade, and with religious toleration. The arbitrary division of Europe into equal Powers was manifestly impossible. The ensuing centuries were to pursue incessantly the Balance of Power, but by ways which repudiated arbitration and left little room for the encouragement of freedom of trade.

So Europe settled down to a " state of nature " not unlike that described by Hobbes; but the parties to the endless warfare were not individuals, but nations. They made no universal contract to obey a common sovereign, but only truces and treaties, which they broke as convenience dictated. Machiavelli ruled. As science developed, the warfare of this " State of Nature " became more effective, that is, more destructive. In the years just after a specially violent paroxysm it did

certainly seem that in the " State of Nature "
" the life of man is nasty, poor, . . .
brutish and short "; and in the Covenant of
the League of Nations the States entered into
a contract which has more resemblance to that
described by Hobbes or Locke or Rousseau
than any agreement to be found in the origins
of any national State. There had been
approaches to this before, notably at Vienna
in 1914. But that was an Alliance; this is
a Confederation; and with the League of
Nations a new hope is born.

In the last Lecture we found that in a true
sense the father of modern politics is Althusius.
If we go back to him for light on the problems
of the internal relations of the State, in dealing
with its external relations we must go back
to another writer whose genius was stimulated
by the supreme achievement of the Netherlands in the sixteenth century—Grotius (1583–
1643). The great Spanish Jesuits had desider-
ated a system of International Law. But
they had not been able to supply a basis for
it other than to indicate that it must be
found in natural law or common reason.
Suarez had been quite clear that however

complete and sovereign a nation may be in its own territory, yet when viewed in relation to the human race it must be regarded, and should regard itself, as a member of that wider unity. The difficulty of the appeal to natural law is at once apparent when we remember that Grotius in its name proclaimed in his *Mare Liberum* the freedom of the seas, as against that Papal grant of the monopoly of Western trade to Spain and Eastern to Portugal, which Suarez was presumably bound to uphold, while Selden wrote the *Mare Clausum* in vindication of England's natural claim to any sovereignty over her own narrow seas that she could exercise.

Grotius was a strong upholder of the doctrine of sovereignty within the State. But his chief title to fame is his work on the problem of the relations of States to one another. He takes his stand first and foremost on Natural Law and Natural Justice. With great ingenuity he argues that the admitted *right* of the sovereign to make war implies already a system of rights—a *jus gentium*—as between sovereign States. And in plain point of fact it is by no means only in recent years that belligerents

have protested the justice of their cause—
thereby committing themselves to a belief
in international justice of some kind. It is
hard to believe that the sort of arguments
advanced by prelates and peers at the beginning of Shakespeare's *Henry V* had any great
influence on the course of events; but Shakespeare plainly thought that they were the
sort of thing that national leaders said to each
other and to the world at large when they
were contemplating an aggression on a neigh-
bouring country.[1] Thus the principle of international right is admitted, and when men go
to war they are always sure that they do it
for their rights. It is only in recent times
that men have begun to perceive how irrelevant
their plea is to their action and their action to
their plea.

What natural law, according to Grotius,
requires is that you may inflict on your enemy
such injury as is required for winning a just
war, and no more. Grotius knew of the
horrors of the Dutch rising against Spain.

---

[1] I never can make up my mind whether Shakespeare
regarded his *Henry V* as a satire or not. If it is a satire,
it is triumphant; if not, it is a calamity. But I wonder.

The Thirty Years War, which had just begun, was to drive home his lesson. In his prolegomena to the *De Jure Belli ac Pacis* he writes : " I saw prevailing throughout the Christian world a licence in making war of which even barbarous nations would be ashamed; recourse being had to arms for slight reasons or no reason; and when arms were once taken up, all reverence for divine and human law was thrown away, just as if men were thenceforth authorised to commit all crimes without restraint." [1] Many of us are ready to echo part at least of that complaint. Grotius would seek first to bridle the passions of war by a declaration that any outrage not conducing to victory is to be condemned. But to this requirement of Natural Justice he adds a Christian principle, which he variously names charity, modesty, or equity and human kindness. This is very moderately conceived and appears chiefly to demand that we should not inflict more injury on an enemy than is likely to be compensated by the good we expect to gain. This is virtually

---

[1] Quoted by R. H. Murray, *The History of Political Science*, p. 191.

the principle of " the greatest happiness of the greatest number," as it was afterwards stated and handled by Hutcheson. It is certainly a very moderate demand, but a nation that knows what war is in itself and in its consequences may easily think it enough to turn the balance altogether from war to arbitration. This was the conclusion to which Grotius wished to point, especially for Christian States : *Maxime autem Christiani reges et civitates tenentur hanc inire viam ad arma vitanda.*

The consideration of profit and loss may be a relatively mean one when questions of honour are alleged to be at stake. But even a purely economic loss, suffered by a nation, is always in its effects something more than economic. The impoverishment of a modern nation brings with it bad trade and unemployment; unemployment involves for those primarily affected a helpless misery, with increasing loss of aptitude for any skilled work, resulting with some in sheer degradation, with others in fierce embitterment. The souls of men suffer through the economic loss attached even to victory in the justest war. If we are to balance the injury done to the enemy by the benefit secured to ourselves in the event of victory, can it ever be right, or even sensible, to engage in war?

In principle, the answer must be No, except where the quarrel is none of our own; but that exception is an important one; and before forming a judgment on any particular case we must take all the circumstances into account. We cannot here do more than glance at some of the principles involved by way of indicating the temper and method which the inquiry demands.

First, then, we recognise several differences between individual and national disputes.

(a) Individuals involved in a dispute are required to submit their case to a court of justice, not to settle it by violence. This is possible because there exists that General Will which constitutes the Community and endows the State with authority.[1] The Court acts for the State and represents the Community, of which the State is an organ, and the resources of the Community are available to uphold the decision of the Court. Here the sense of the Community comes first; therefore the defeated

[1] See Lecture III. pp. 119–123.

individual accepts the verdict. Even if he
thinks it unjust he accepts it, either because
he really prefers the authority of the State to
his own interest, or because he knows that in
fact he is powerless against the State, or for
both these reasons at once.

But in international disputes there has been,
till lately, nothing corresponding to the State
or its Courts to act for the international Community. Therefore when a dispute arose there
was no arbitrator who could enforce his
award. It was difficult to choose an arbitrator;
everyone who was competent was likely to
have some reason for inclining one way or the
other. But the real difficulty was the lack of
security that the other party would accept the
award if it went against him. That was a
weakness about the Hague Tribunal which
incapacitated it for service in cases where
hostile passions, with suspicion among them,
were deeply stirred. To take an illustration :
it would have been ideally right that Bismarck
and Napoleon III should have submitted their
case to arbitration in 1870; but in the actual
conditions it would have betrayed a Utopian
disregard of human passions to expect it;

there was not even a Hague Tribunal in those days.

(b) The national State acts for a community which is, as Burke reminded his contemporaries, a partnership of many generations, including those yet unborn. The State of our generation, therefore, has not the same right to sacrifice the essential interests of its community as an individual has to sacrifice his own. I remember hearing a nobly consistent pacifist woman asked during the days of the Great War what she would have done on August 4, 1914. The questioner hoped to jeer at one who should propose in the name of Christianity that we should sit safely by while the world agonised, mopping up the trade of the belligerents. But the pacifist woman answered : " I should have sunk the Navy." Noble, as I said. But, I am sure, not right. To have left the world to lie prostrate before a triumphant military despotism, quite apart from all questions of promises previously made, would have been an injury to other nations; it would have been treachery to our own descendants.

Those who wish to protest against some

action of the State often employ the maxim: What is morally wrong cannot be politically right. This is true if it means that it cannot be politically right for the State to do what it is morally wrong for the State to do. But that is not usually what is meant. This maxim is usually intended, by those who make use of it, to declare that it cannot be right for the State to do what it would be wrong for an individual to do; and this is completely untrue. It shows a complete misunderstanding of the ethical problem to suppose that certain acts are right and certain other acts are wrong quite irrespective of the agent who does them and of the circumstances in which they are done. If that were the state of affairs, ethics would be a very much simpler science than it is. Broadly speaking I suppose it is wrong for me to hit a man on the head with a poker; but if he is a burglar who has broken into my house and is covering my wife with a revolver, it may be quite right. The difficulty of decision arises with reference to border-line cases, where it is not clear on which side of the line the right is to be found; and this most often happens when there are real claims

Hugh Price Hughes.

tending in opposite directions, but these are of different kinds so that they cannot be properly weighed against each other.

A good illustration is provided by the decision which the British Government had to make in August 1914. On the one side was the suffering that war would entail, the loss to the community of invaluable lives, the economic impoverishment and all the horrors involved in it, and the almost certain degradation of moral character on a great scale—only to be averted, in all probability, by military defeat. On the other side was the sanctity of a promise given, the claim of a small nation (Belgium) to have its effective independence protected, the obligation to safeguard the political influence of freedom and justice against aggressive force and despotism. No doubt the Government was also concerned about that balance of power in Europe which always ministers to our importance among the nations. But the fact that a lower—not actually evil, but lower—consideration played its part, does not affect the other fact that choice had to be made between the two groups of considerations already mentioned,

The grounds on which it was made affect the moral quality of the agents; it is the relative merits of the two groups of considerations themselves, which alone decide the moral quality of the act. For a good act may be done by a bad man, or by a good man for bad reasons, as well as by a good man for good reasons. It is, as a matter of fact, a result of our geographical position that it always serves our interest to uphold international justice in Europe. This is one source of the accusation of hypocrisy constantly levelled against us. Our neighbours see that we are serving our own interests. We prefer to concentrate attention on the more flattering consideration that we are upholding justice. The fact that a just act is profitable does not make it other than just, but it does remove its character as occasion for moral self-gratulation.

It may safely be said that to enter on war as the culmination of a selfish policy is always wrong; but the causative wrong is the selfish policy. Whether a war of sheer self-defence is right or wrong is harder to determine. A nation which was ready to suffer annihilation rather than stain its soul with the passion of war might save both itself and others. But the State which embarks on such a policy must be sure that it carries with it the whole nation, the community. Trustees have no right to inflict self-sacrifice on their clients. And it may be safely anticipated that no nation could reach that height of self-sacrifice till other nations were so near to the same height that the actual risk of annihilation would be nil. The system of mutual influence in which the characters of men are determined is not likely to allow the emergence of a martyr-nation. And it is by no means certain that the martyr-nation would be right. Not only is the State a trustee for the community, but each national community is a trustee for the world-wide community, to which it should bring treasures of its own; and to submit to political annihilation may be to defraud mankind of what it alone could have contributed to the general wealth of human experience.

It is not by confusing the proper conduct of a State with the proper conduct of an individual that good-will may be promoted and peace may be secured. The essential problems of the two are quite different. Quite different also are the principles governing the internal and the external relations of States. The business of the State with regard to its own community is to maintain the unity that exists while making room for an increasing development of personality within it, or the fostering of individuality without injury to the unity of society. Its task in relation to other States is the precise opposite; it is the creation and strengthening of a community of nations without injury to their individuality, or the safeguarding of their individuality while fostering the community. Within the nation, unity (broadly speaking) is given; the problem is to foster independence; among the nations, independence is given and the problem is to foster unity.

Among the data for the solution of this problem are the actual psychological factors. For centuries loyalty has been directed primarily to the national State; any proposal which violently conflicts with that ingrained emotional habit is bound to fail. Moreover, it ought to fail, because the national State, or the national community which has grown up under its protection, is the best actual achievement of the principle of fellowship up to date. The Bolshevik effort to unite men internationally on the basis of economic interests against other groups similarly based is definitely retrograde, because the unity of a nation is far richer in content than the unity of an economic class, and its fellowship is proportionately more valuable. The values won in the nationalist phase of history must not be lost as we consciously and definitely enter on the international.

Our effort, then, must be to find what light is thrown by the nature of the State itself and the logic of its development upon the problem of its relations with other States. It is here that the doctrine of the State as fundamentally resting on force is so disastrous, for it encourages the national egoism which leads to the self-assertion of the State against its neighbours. It derives some support from the actual behaviour of States; it coheres with the doctrine of State-absolutism which observance of that behaviour prompted. But it is demonstrably false. The art of bullying and the art of governing are manifestly not the same. The force entrusted to the State is, as we saw in the last Lecture, the sign and guarantee of the universality of Law, Law (not force) being the actual mark of the State, and the General Will for a community its ultimate ground; and force is confined to the State precisely in order that it may always be used under the control and for the maintenance of Law. " Force," says MacIver finely, " saves us only from itself. Men praise the ' sword ' because it gives them victory over the ' sword,' or delivers them from defeat. In each country they chant pæans over the armed forces which protect them— each country from the other." [1] Our habit of thinking only from the point of view of our own country prevents us from seeing how ludicrous this is. But if we take Europe as our unit, how absurd is this glorification of the instruments of self-destruction! If we take the Kingdom of God as the object of our ultimate allegiance, how treasonous is the exaltation of the means of self-aggrandise-ment at the cost of others! But this last

[1] *The Modern State*, p. 228.

is a matter we shall have to consider later on.

It is very commonly held that the State is most of all itself when dealing with other States; and the ground for this conviction is that its absolute sovereignty is then most apparent. There are, moreover, two ways in which foreign relations appear to exhibit this Sovereignty in a special degree. First, those relationships themselves exhibit the fact that the State acknowledges no superior. It does not ask leave to make its decisions or to act on them; nor will it brook interference. Secondly, it is recognised to have the right to call on its citizens to obey its commands even to the death. What are we to say with regard to such claims?

I take the second first, because it is the most often challenged, and I believe it to be in principle beyond dispute. It is perfectly true that in war the State compels all other interests of men to be subordinated to the political interest. Commerce, culture, family ties—all count as nothing compared with the exigencies of State. This constitutes a great temptation. The statesman, like other human beings, is prone to magnify his office and to see life habitually in the perspectives apparent from the State's point of view; to him the sacrifice of all these other interests to the State is only an expression of the true order of their importance. This is one reason among very many why it is unsafe to be governed by statesmen to whom politics are the primary personal interest. It is well that they should be men who personally care more for other pursuits and administer the State from a sense of duty. No man who revels in power can safely be entrusted with it. In the claim of the State to use and sacrifice its citizens in its cause there is a fearful peril. And yet the claim, in principle, is just. The State is the only necessary organ of the community. The loss of any of its specialised associations would be an impoverishment; the collapse of the State is likely, at least, to break up the community itself. This is not necessary; it is possible to destroy the State and reconstruct it without destroying the community; but even so the loss is fearful. The State, as the organ of national unity, is so closely bound up with the com-

M

munity that it has almost as irresistible a claim as the community itself.[1]   The political interest of men is not in itself so precious as their social and cultural interests; but it is in a special sense indispensable to these. Therefore the State is, in principle, entitled to subordinate these to itself for a sufficient reason; and it is, in principle, justified in calling on its citizens to die, and even to kill, for the preservation of what is necessary to it as the indispensable instrument of the nation's life.

There are many subsidiary considerations to be added in this connection, but they do not affect the main point. We pass to the first claim mentioned above—the claim that the State supremely exhibits its inherent sovereignty in foreign relations, because here, where it deals with its equals, it submits to no superior.   This claim is commonly admitted to be valid; I believe it to be entirely false. Of course it is beyond question that States have acted on this claim, so that a theory

---

[1] Of course this does not mean that *the Government* always has this claim; but when the Government administers the State against the welfare of the community the normally right course is to turn it out, not to resist it while it remains the Government.

which erects it into a principle is not to be refuted by historical facts. My contention is that the State in so acting has not exhibited, but has concealed, its true nature.

First we must notice that this theory depends for its plausibility on our adopting the national point of view. As soon as we take a European or broadly human point of view this claim to sovereignty appears just like the claim to total independence put forward by Hobbes on behalf of his imaginary human beings in the state of nature. Each was sovereign, and for that very reason life became unbearable for each and all. So since the Renaissance every State in Europe has claimed to be sovereign; its sovereignty is chiefly exhibited (the claim maintains) in the right to make war or peace. Many of us are beginning to feel that as a direct result of this precious sovereignty, " the life of man is . . . poor, nasty, brutish and short." In other words, the claim to sovereignty in this sense is, through the very exercise of sovereignty, leading to its own repudiation. That strongly suggests that the claim is false in principle.

Secondly, we have seen that the State is an organ of community and exists to serve its community. But what conceivable issue can arise the solution of which by arbitration would not better serve the community than the arbitrament of war? It is said that we cannot be sure of an impartial tribunal. Is war, then, so conspicuously impartial? When a dispute arose between Prussia and Denmark, in 1863, and each side held that the interests at stake were vital, is it so certain that that bloodiest of idols, the God of Battles, decided the issue according to justice? Is not that particular idol a notorious coward, always siding with the big battalions? [1] This cant about the partiality of any international tribunal is peculiarly nauseating. Of course we cannot secure complete impartiality. We have not got it in the English Courts of Justice, nor in any tribunal that has been or can be set up on earth; but we know that it is better to let the courts decide than to appeal from them to force which does not even aim at impartiality or justice but only

[1] The fact that God can bring good out of evil is no reason for attributing evil directly to God's action.

at " superiority." We are told that we could not submit to arbitration " vital interests " or " questions of honour." But there can be few interests which do not suffer more through a victorious war than from a hostile award. And what honour is that which is satisfied by our divesting ourselves of the human and god-like faculty of reason that we may impose or accept the judgment of a force which is only not brutal because, being intellectually directed, it is devilish ? So far as the State acts for its national community, it will always serve it best by resorting to arbitration, and by taking every possible step to forward such international arrangements as may secure that in all cases of dispute arbitration takes the place of war. Till those arrangements are completed, war may be a duty; but to complete them is as certainly a duty.

But, thirdly, it is when we consider the State as acting distinctively by law that we see how truly the logic of its own nature presses it on towards international organisation. After all, the State, we found, possesses force as the means of upholding the universality of law;

and force is confined to the State in order that it may only be exercised under the control, and for the maintenance, of law. But war is the repudiation of law. If the State goes to war in preference to accepting arbitration, it follows its mere property of force in preference to its essential characteristic of law. It is not then most of all itself; on the contrary it is then false to itself. It shows its true nature when it promotes that international organisation which will secure the reign of law (its own true essence) in international relations.

Progress in this matter is being made, but it is long overdue. We find a fourth compelling reason for action in this direction in the relation of the State to the various associations through which men pursue the various interests of life. These grew up, we saw, within the national community; but the self-contained character of that community was an accident of history; it was due to the fact that, when means of communication were meagre, intercourse was geographically limited. We may well be glad of this, for it facilitated the development of a variety of national types. But it remains true that the national character of most human associations was always accidental. As soon as the external cause for this limitation of association was removed, all manner of international associations, economic, cultural and religious, sprang into effective life. This is one reason why modern war is so incomparably disastrous. It involves a reversion to the purely national point of view. When the nation comprised most human interests and activities there was comparatively little harm in this. Now it is a calamity beyond estimate. As the international ties are drawn closer, the opportunities of friction increase as well as those of friendship; and because all nations are linked together, none can stand aloof. The disparity between an international society and purely national States both precipitated the World War and added to its horrors. " The age of competitive armaments and competitive alliances culminated in the World War. . . . The struggle could not be localised because the nations were so interdependent, so bound up with one another. All the great nations of the world were embroiled . . . because a single system held them fast. Nothing was common save the catastrophe. In the words of Viscount Grey, ' it was a victory of war itself over everybody who took part in it.' The significance of this fact is simply that war has become an anachronism, an institution incompatible with the civilisation which has overspread the world." [1]

And yet, as things were, it is hard to see how the new age could have dawned without the War. Men's political theory was in all nations so far removed from the actual facts of the new world that it is doubtful if they would have abandoned their idolatrous State-absolutism if it had not manifestly led them to calamity. Moreover, the whole conception of the State which finds its natural expression

---

[1] MacIver, *The Modern State*, pp. 247–8. But I cannot agree with the words in this passage which I have omitted. They run : " a monstrous struggle without intrinsic purpose, involving nation after nation in a conflict whose initial issues were obscure to them and irrelevant to their interests. Mankind has never witnessed so tragic a disparity between means and ends "— and later, after " embroiled "—" not because a single issue divided them, but——" My grounds for rejecting these words will be apparent from what follows in the text.

under modern conditions in the League of Nations is the extreme antithesis of that which had inspired Prussia since the time of Frederick the Great, or Austria from the time of the Thirty Years War, and it is almost inconceivable that a true League of Nations could have been inaugurated until the military monarchies of those States had been overthrown. The same is true of pre-revolutionary Russia. But history had made it necessary that the genesis of any League that was to work successfully should be among the Western European nations who had inherited that respect for law, which ancient Rome gave those who were fortunate enough to be conquered by her. A shrewd German observer said near the beginning of the war that it was a struggle between *Kultur* and the ideas of 1789. Fundamentally that is true, though the men of 1789, bemused by Rousseau, had so confused those ideas that it is often hard to disentangle them. The war was a struggle between the idea of the State as essentially Power—Power over its own community and against other communities—and of the State as the organ of community, maintaining its solidarity by law designed to safeguard the interests of the community. The Power-State might have yielded to sheer pressure of circumstances in course of time; but it is contrary to the psychology of the Power-State to suffer conversion; it was likely to fight before it let a Welfare-State take its place. After all, it cost England two revolutions to reach the ideas of John Locke, unsystematic as they were; and it cost France another, equivalent in convulsiveness to our two put together, to secure ascendancy for the ideas of 1789. The Power-States of Austria and Prussia were not likely to yield to anything but power. The great objective issue in the war, vital for all peoples, was the issue between two theories of the State. It was no accident that the Italy of Mazzini and Cavour dropped out of the Triple Alliance to become the ally of French and British democracy; nor was it an accident that its place by the side of the military empires was taken by Turkey. If it is true, as I think it is, that " the establishment of a League of Nations, directed towards the abolition of competitive armaments and the judicial settlement of international disputes, is not so much the institutional expression of an ideal as the belated adjustment of an institution to realities," [1] then it is also true that, before this adjustment could be made, the Power-State had to be swept into the limbo of forgotten idolatries. The issue of the victory of the Allies in the establishment of the League was no accident; it was the logical outcome of the principles which differentiated their political life from that of their opponents. Nothing is now so important as that the champions of those principles should be loyal to them.

The whole of this argument may be summed up very briefly. The State is an organ of community; community has mainly been territorially demarcated into nations; therefore the State has been national. Community is become very largely international; therefore the State must become international also.

We have found that the essential nature of the State and the immanent logic of its own development points towards the realisation of

[1] MacIver, *The Modern State*, p. 249.

an international State, an organ of the international community as the existing State is of the national community, promulgating law and possessed of force by which to secure for that law its essential characteristic of universality. But this international State will not be found already existing by the mere process of differentiating from it the other interests of mankind. It has to be deliberately constructed. There is need for a real Social Contract between the nations to lift them from the state of nature to the level of civilised community. Such a contract was never made by primitive mankind to found society or the State; but it was made in the Covenant of 1919 to found the League of Nations.

The League involves no supersession of the nation. The variety of the nations is good. A non-national cosmopolitanism, which would depreciate national distinctions, would thereby also abolish many valuable elements of our experience. But we can learn to rejoice in each other's peculiarities instead of detesting them. Only Germany could have given us Goethe; only Russia Dostoievski; only England Browning. Each can rejoice in the products of the others. We have to rise above the stupid alternative of identity and antagonism, of unison and discord, and help both to create and to enjoy harmony.

It still remains to ask how the argument that we have outlined is related to Christian principles. The doctrine of State-absolutism, at any rate, cannot be Christian, for it ignores or defies the sole absolute sovereignty of God. To Him the obedience of the State is due, as is that of all things in the created world. Before Him there are no rights which are not also duties. The State for a Christian may have the right to determine for itself what is its duty to God at a given time; it has no right to do anything except in accordance with His sovereign Will. When Italy was considering whether or not to enter the Great War, statesmen and editors combined to say that of course she must determine the matter according to her own interest. That is false, unless indeed by " interest " is meant her highest spiritual interest; and the way to serve that is to seek no interest at all, but only duty. Italy had no right to enter the war unless it was her duty to enter the war, just as we had no right to enter it unless it was our duty. I believe that, in all the conditions of that time, it was our duty; and if the conditions were repeated, it would be our duty again. For it was not a war of aggression, nor even (in the mind of the people at least) of self-defence. It was a war to keep our promise, to protect the independence of a small nation, and to secure not so much predominance as continued existence for "the ideas of 1789" against an embattled *Kultur* already in arms against them. But though it would be again our duty to go to war if the same conditions were repeated, it is still more obviously our duty to see that those conditions never are repeated. That they existed at all was due to sin in our pre-war civilisation. Among nations that were Christian in all their dealings there could be no thought of war.

The Christian's ultimate loyalty is due, not to his earthly State, but to the Kingdom of God, wherein all nations are provinces. If his loyalty to God conflicts with his loyalty to the State, it is the former that must prevail. The modern respect for "conscientious objection" to what the State requires, whether that be military service or some other action which the conscience of an individual may condemn, is a great sign of progress. No doubt the poor human "conscience" is invoked in relation to many matters with which philosophers will say that it has nothing at all to do; this is only one more illustration of the truth that man is not a rational animal, but only an animal striving to become rational. The fact remains that for the State to respect "conscientious objection" is a recognition on its part that its citizens have a duty to something other and higher than itself, which Christians will call the Kingdom of God.

I do not share the conscientious objection felt by many to military service. I believe the State, when acting for the community, has a right to call upon me to be killed and even to kill in support of its cause, if that cause be just and can only be upheld by war. But the State has no right to call upon me to hate its enemies. There are those who have sneered at the fact that in the war men were more willing to give their lives than their property. But there is nothing to sneer about. It was only their animal lives—their mortal bodies—that they gave. Property is an expression of personality and is valued accordingly. Often it is valued blindly and foolishly, but it is not a purely blind valuation which prefers property, which can become the expression of personality for generations unborn, to the physical life which is anyhow bound to end before long. Yet the State has a claim on my property as well as on my body. But upon my character it has no claim. That belongs first and foremost to God and to eternity; and the State can only secure good service from it by recognising that it must not direct it. Those men best serve the State who are ready, if occasion come, in God's name to defy the State.

Now all experience shows that human nature has never in the mass so far appropriated the Grace of God that it can pass through the horrors of war with character unstained, even though to enter the war was at the time the only course of duty. If the argument for providing against war is strong on grounds of economic interest, on moral grounds it is overwhelming. To organise for peace is a most manifest Christian duty. And if we find, as we have found, that the very nature of the State presses us in this direction for the fulfilment of its own destiny, we cannot be in any doubt where the course of Christian statesmanship lies. It is the way of progressive international federation—the way of the League of Nations.

Perhaps it is still worth while to explode that hoary delusion which expresses itself in the Latin tag—*Si vis pacem, para bellum*— If you wish for peace, prepare for war. That was a quite sensible maxim as applied to the Roman Empire. The Empire comprised the whole civilised world; it had natural frontiers all round it—the ocean, the Rhine, the Danube, the mountains of Asia Minor, the Euphrates, the Desert. If such an empire were prepared for war, no one would make war upon it. The circumstances which made that maxim sensible were the very opposite of our system of competitive armaments. For us the sensible maxim has less literary attractiveness; it is—If you wish for peace, prepare for peace.

This preparation must be conducted along three channels: educational, political, re-

N

ligious. Education for peace will not mean peace propaganda in the schools; it will only mean the substitution of scientific completeness for patriotic bias. I remember that when I was about twelve years old I was greatly puzzled by the fact that there was only Calais left to be engraved on poor Queen Mary's heart as she lay a-dying. I had been told about Crécy, and Poitiers, and Agincourt; I had learnt by heart a speech about St. Crispin's day, which had a jolly eagerness in it; I had heard of our Henry VI being crowned King of France. But I had heard nothing of the campaigns in which the British armies were driven out of France. Somehow all our conquests, except Calais, were gone; but they never told me how. I seem to have heard something about Joan of Arc, but she appeared as a strange and isolated episode. Apparently I was only to be told of English victories. In 1917 (I think it was) I came across a French nursery-history of France. It mentioned Agincourt, but did not dignify it with the name of a battle; it was " an engagement "— " discreditable to French arms because our forces, though more numerous, were defeated."

Then followed page after page describing the glorious campaigns in which the soil of France was liberated from the invading foreigner.

Now this sort of thing will not do. Of course the history taught to children must consist of selections. But the principle of the selection should be an aspiration towards scientific truth, not a desire to glorify a particular country. We do not need propaganda; we do need to insist that whatever episode is taught should be taught in its complete outline as far as may be. And we should aim at such knowledge as most helps us to understand the origin of the world with which we have to do. English children hear a great deal about Henry V of England, whose performances were, in fact, singularly unimportant except in evoking the national spirit of France; they hear next to nothing about his really important cousin, Henry the Navigator, Prince of Portugal. But the opening of the high seas to commerce is something which can easily be grasped by children, and its importance is incalculable. We must give our energies to implanting in children from the beginning the European—even the human

—point of view, not as substituting one bias for another, but as trying to avoid all partiality and bias so far as human beings may.

With this must go the political preparation for peace, the deliberate fulfilment by the State of the law of its own being by its subjection of Force to Law in international as in domestic matters, with the double object that law may be universal in its scope and that force may never be used except in its service and for its maintenance. To this end it seems most desirable that every State should sign the so-called "Optional Clause" of the Statute of the Permanent Court of International Justice, thereby accepting the jurisdiction of the Permanent Court for the settlement of all disputes of a legal character with any other States which had also signed this clause. Further, every State should be willing to conclude with any other States arbitration treaties providing for the peaceful settlement of international disputes of every kind.

The establishment of the Permanent Court is, next to the inauguration of the League itself, the most hopeful symptom of the new era. The great difficulty about disputes between nations is that of finding a referee who not only is impartial, but whose impartiality is believed in by both disputants. A Permanent Court may not be perfectly impartial; perhaps no human tribunal can be; if the New Psychology is to be trusted, the fairest judge is at the mercy of influences which he cannot check because he is unaware of their existence. But a Court established as a permanent institution in connection with the League and its representative Assembly has a greater prospect not only of being impartial but also (which is even more important) of being accepted as impartial, than any other tribunal previously established or proposed. The greater the number of States that acknowledge it, the greater will be not only the authority, but the impartiality of the Court, for there will always be pressing upon it the need to retain the confidence of all whom it exists to serve.

This introduces a principle of the utmost importance. If international bodies, whether deliberative or judicial, are to make for peace, they must be invested with authority. Men like to achieve something in return for trouble taken. If when they are brought together there is nothing to be done except that one side or another wins a debate, they will emphasise points of difference; if by reaching an agreement they can settle a dispute, they will emphasise points of unity. Therefore whenever men representing different States come together with power to act, they will promote peace; but to bring them together without power to act is to intensify the causes of war. But that is not all. When they are thus come together with power to act, all settlements must be worked out in the full assembly or in its accredited committees. There should be no secret planning by a few States behind closed doors, in order that they may propose a policy on which they are agreed and to which, for that reason, the rest must willy-nilly agree on pain of breaking up the assembly or rendering its meeting futile. If on some given occasion the existing suspicions and jealousies of States make such a course inevitable, that must be recognised as an abnormal and unwholesome condition. The historic secrecy of diplomacy has its roots in suspicion and its fruits in ill-will.

What has just been said was not intended to refer only to the League of Nations, its Assembly, and its Council, but it plainly has a a very special application there. The League itself is a mere piece of machinery; the amount of work that it can do must be largely determined by the motive-power supplied to it. This can only come from the desire of the peoples that the general welfare should prevail as against their particular interests. But this implies real conversion on a great scale. It is not natural to man to prefer the general good to his own; indeed that is a description of what in one word is called salvation. Along with the educational and the political preparation for peace must go the religious preparation also—the inculcation of an absolute loyalty to God and His Justice in His all-embracing Kingdom, and the deliberate checking of all narrower loyalties by that. The failure of our religion to accomplish the great things it promises is a failure of our expectation. For the power of God works in us through our faith; and the form which faith takes in relation to the promises of God as yet unfulfilled is expectation. When we truly expect, as the result of our prayers and of our reception of the Universal Humanity of Christ in our communions, that we shall rise above suspicions and jealousies and co-operate trustfully in promoting the common good, that blessing will come to us. And when enough citizens are Christian in their citizenship, the State they uphold will become a Christian State.

But so we come to the most specifically Christian demand that we are to make of the State. "Do you really mean," says the objector, "that the Sovereign-State should hand over to an international assembly the determination of its own policy in matters affecting its own interest?" Yes: we do mean precisely that; and we maintain that this alone is the fulfilment of true sovereignty inasmuch as the securing of the reign of Law throughout the world is the fulfilment of the true nature of the State. For the archetypal sovereignty is that of God; and when God was incarnate among men He said, "I am among you as he that serveth." At a moment when Christ was specially conscious of His divine authority and mission, He did not sit on a throne and demand the homage of His subjects or the submission of His enemies; He rendered to His disciples a specially menial service.

Service is the only true dignity. To obey is as noble as to command, to command as noble as to obey, if each is done as an act of service in the allotted sphere; otherwise there is no dignity in either. The Christian can be as true a patriot as any other; he can desire for his country the foremost place with an equal zeal. The difference is in the standard or scale of values. The foremost place that he will desire for his country is the place of foremost service to God and to His Kingdom. The State is concerned with law; it cannot be, as the Church ought to be, a spiritual pioneer; its function is to consolidate the moral gains already won and save us from falling below the normal level of our own achievement. Hence it must be firm and even stern in its action. Its way of manifesting love is to be just, and there are other and higher ways. But the State which has learnt its true function has, none the less, the highest of earthly dignities; it is an indispensable servant of the common life of men. Its form of service is to rule; but it should rule only that it may serve.

APPENDIX I

Some Notes on Dr. Raven's " The Creator Spirit "

DR. RAVEN is rightly eager to maintain the supremacy of love, and seems to fear that some others, who agree with him in this, are following lines of argument that lead elsewhere. In this sense he criticises an argument of my own. I trust that I have never said anything to suggest that we should " relegate Will to the Creator and Love to the Incarnate."[1] For one thing, the Word which was incarnate is itself the agent of Creation. Dr. Raven's book is in general so admirable, and I anticipate for it so great an influence, that I think it may be worth while to outline here the grounds of my disagreement with some of its positions. He appears to misunderstand the thought of those whom he is here criticising through failure to grasp the fact that it rests on a " critical " argument, not on either a deductive or on an inductive argument. He

[1] *Op. cit.*, p. 103.

complains of Dr. D'Arcy and myself for maintaining that the ground of the Universe must
be Will, saying that there are not enough
instances of teleological adaptation to support
this view. He writes : " If every particle of
every creature was what it was because it
served some definable purpose, and if the
formulation of this purpose was the chief end
of biology, then naturally the Christian would
lay supreme stress upon teleology and conclude
that ' if we ask for an explanation of the
universe as a whole, we are bound to formulate
the answer in terms of will.' "[1] But the
argument would be equally valid if there
were no such instances at all. The argument
is that the only principle known to us which
is capable of giving an ultimate explanation
of anything at all is Will or Purpose; there
may be proximate explanations of all particular
things; but of the Whole there is either an
ultimate explanation or no explanation at all.
Therefore the explanation of the Whole must
be sought in Will or nowhere.

Dr. Raven writes : " Dr. Temple would not,

[1] *Op. cit.*, p. 103. The quotation is from my book,
Christus Veritas, p. 7.

I think, have written : ' If we ask for an explanation of Jesus Christ, we are bound to formulate the answer in terms of Will.' " If I had succeeded in making my argument clear to him, he would have seen that I should quite readily say precisely that. But of course it is true that the Will which expresses itself in Jesus Christ is not just any Will; it is a Will which is perfect Love.

This brings us to a second source of confusion, as I think, in Dr. Raven's argument. He finds the ground of the Universe in Love, which he sharply distinguishes from Will; and I cannot see how Love apart from Will (if I knew what that meant at all) could be in itself creative. So far as Love is creative, it is because Love is a determination of Will. Perhaps the matter may be put in this way : *quâ* Will, God is capable of creating; *quâ* Love, He exercises that capacity and actually creates.

While I am referring to Dr. Raven's most stimulating and interesting book I should like to say that what he calls the Spirit is for the most part what I call the Logos. The Spirit (I hold) is properly that power of God in the heart which is elicited by the Incarnation. Hence the home of the Spirit is the Church, and He sanctifies, not all men, but the elect—that is, those who are privileged to receive the revelation of God in Christ. As a result of identifying, or (as I think) confusing, the Spirit with the Logos, Dr. Raven seems to me to represent Jesus Christ as first and foremost the supreme manifestation of the Spirit and hardly at all as, for us, the source of the Spirit; in traditional theology He is both, but the second thought predominates. Congruously with this view the Church appears in Dr. Raven's scheme, as I apprehend it, as one channel of the Spirit among many, rather than as the normal channel which His influence overflows to permeate all human activities.

Let me repeat that I indicate these points of difference precisely because I so greatly admire Dr. Raven's work as a whole, and desire, as I expect, that many should read it and receive its stimulus; for this reason I think it worth while to indicate, for the further stimulus of thought in any who read both that book and this, the chief points where I am unable to follow him.

APPENDIX II

On the Relations Between Church and State

THE rejection by the House of Commons of the Prayer Book Measure in the December of 1927 suddenly raised again one of the chief permanent problems of European political philosophy. With the special merits of that Measure and the action of Parliament we are not now concerned. But we are very much concerned with the political principles involved.

The fact that Parliament has authority over the Church's law of public worship is an historical accident; it has nothing to do with " Establishment " as such. In Scotland the Reformation was Calvinist in principle and popular in origin; both of these characteristics would have tended to secure for the General Assembly of the Kirk complete spiritual autonomy. The Church of Scotland is as much " established " as the Church of England; the King is supreme; but the Royal Supremacy operates, as regards spiritual matters, through the Assembly and not through Parliament. The English Reformation was (in all relevant aspects) Lutheran in principle and Governmental in origin; both facts tended towards an Erastian constitution. But in the days of Henry VIII, Edward VI, Elizabeth, and Charles II, when the various stages of the English Reformation settlement were effected, Parliament was itself an assembly of churchmen representing churchmen, though on a civic and not an ecclesiastical basis.

Since then the advent of religious toleration has turned Parliament into an assembly consisting of persons of all manner of religious opinions and representing persons of all manner of religious opinions. No one would deliberately entrust to Parliament as now constituted the acceptance or rejection of proposals for the revision of the Prayer Book. The situation is an anomalous result of an historic process.

In 1919 a modification of the Constitution was adopted whereby an Assembly created by the Church was empowered by Parliament to frame legislative Measures which Parliament would then accept or reject by a single resolution in each of the two Houses. This arrangement was made because Parliament could not give the necessary time for ecclesiastical legislation. The Church was greatly hampered through inability to make changes in its legal system, an inability due, as far as was known, not to Parliamentary hostility but to lack of Parliamentary time. It is important to remember that the National Assembly of the Church of England was not in any sense created by Parliament. Its Constitution was drawn up by the Representative Church Council, was approved by the Convocations, and was submitted to the Throne by the Convocations, which have an ancient right of direct approach to the Throne. To the Assembly thus constituted Parliament gave certain powers; but the Constitution is only referred to in the Powers Act; it is not a part of it nor is it a schedule to it.

The legislation of 1919 was admittedly experimental. Many of those who supported it were demanding freedom for the Church to control its own life, " even, if need be, at the cost of disestablishment and of whatever that may involve." Those words appeared in the first manifestoes of the Life and Liberty

Movement. But it was agreed that the proposals already made by the Archbishops' Committee on Church and State should be given a full trial.

The Church Assembly first met in the summer of 1920. In the seven years of its existence it has carried a great amount of legislation. Two of its Measures had been rejected by Parliament before the Prayer Book Measure was presented : the Shrewsbury Bishopric Measure was rejected by one vote in the House of Lords and a Measure for dealing with parishes and churches in the City of London was rejected by the House of Commons. In the former case, one of the two Diocesan Conferences directly concerned was hostile ; in the latter the City itself had a manifest interest, and the City was hostile. Parliament therefore had good grounds for its action. Anyhow, neither of these Measures touched the Church's inner life. In 1927 the Prayer Book Measure was presented ; it had overwhelming support from the Bishops, the Convocations, and the Church Assembly ; the same support was forthcoming from the Diocesan Conferences all over the country.

o

The House of Lords approved the Measure by a very large majority; by a narrow margin the House of Commons rejected it.

What the final upshot may be we have no reason here to prophesy. Parliament is likely before long to have the opportunity of considering the same Measure with a few purely explanatory modifications; and it may then accept it. But questions are raised affecting fundamental principles, the more so because the speeches made in opposition to the Measure in the House of Commons all rested on the convictions of the speakers with regard to the doctrine of the Church of England and the relation of the revised Prayer Book to that doctrine.

Now it is most emphatically not the business of the State to determine what is, and what is not, compatible with theological truth. The State which handles such themes has transgressed the limits of its own province and must be resisted. On the other hand, it is precisely the business of the Church to determine such matters, though those who act for it do well to remember the inadequacy of all human faculties for the task. It is not possible that the Church should allow the State to determine its doctrine or its mode of worship. In 1662 Parliament asserted its constitutional right to override the decisions of the Convocations and then formally determined not to do so; the Prayer Book of 1662 received legislative sanction precisely as it had been drawn up by the Convocations.

Parliament is perfectly within its rights, both legal and moral, in determining whether any Church should be " established " or not. It has a complete legal right, but not (I hold) a moral right, to determine what the Prayer Book of the Established Church shall be. If the theory outlined in these Lectures is sound, the proper course for Parliament to pursue if it disapproves the Prayer Book Measure is not to reject the Measure, but to pass the Measure and then disestablish the Church.

In any case the Church has its own spiritual responsibility ; it cannot hand over to another body the determination of its modes of worship. If Parliament uses its unquestioned legal right to restrict the Church's freedom in this field, the Church must act through its own organs, and leave the State to do what it thinks right.

o *

In actual fact most of the Bishops simply disobeyed the Law.

"The Church of England by representation," according to the Constitution of this realm, is to be found neither in Parliament nor in the Church Assembly, but in the Convocations. Those ancient bodies, more ancient than Parliament itself, may be about to come into their own again. It is desirable that they should work with the Church Assembly, for the laity should take their share in the decisions reached; but the Church has its own spiritual authorities, and they can act if the need arise.

The question of Establishment itself is very difficult in modern conditions. I believe it is good for the State to be (so to speak) affiliated to the Divine Society; and so far as Establishment means this, it is altogether wholesome. If, however, it means a claim by the State to exercise a special degree of control over the Church, it is an anomaly to be abolished as soon as may be. If the Church can win for itself, or the State is willing to bestow upon it, such freedom in spiritual matters as is enjoyed by the Established Presbyterian Church of Scotland, that is probably the best arrangement that can be devised. If the State will not

As it always must

Surely you cannot have the privileges of Establishment without some subtlevitue!

consent to this, at least in practice, whatever theoretical rights of control it retains, then the sooner the Establishment is ended the better.

But it must be remembered that the fundamental question is not that of Establishment at all; the fundamental question is the right of an association within the Community to live its own life. The State is, of necessity, the only authority which can determine to whom property belongs; it has not only the right, but the duty, to do this. If the Church were disestablished it still would not be effectively free if all the instruments of its work— its buildings and the like—were tied up by a Trust Deed to a particular system of doctrine. The great legal case affecting the Free Church of Scotland illustrates this. The House of Lords held in effect that the property of the Free Church of Scotland did not belong to a living body which, because living, might change its opinions, but to certain opinions of which the supporters were so few that they were known as the " Wee Frees "; and Parliament had to pass special legislation to remedy a situation manifestly absurd. It is this indefeasible supremacy of the State in questions of property which gives to the perennial problem of the relations between Church and State its abiding interest. Can there be living societies within the Community ? It is by its strenuous insistence that there can that the Church has rendered its most conspicuous service to the cause of liberty. In upholding its own spiritual autonomy the Church is asserting on behalf of all associations concerned with the higher values, their right to live their own lives; in resisting a State which fails to respect that autonomy, it is serving the Community; and if that resistance involves it in acts of moral rebellion, its rebellion is the expression of its loyalty. The State, which involves in so paradoxical a duty any great association within the Community which it safeguards, is acting contrary to its own true nature.

PRINTED IN GREAT BRITAIN BY RICHARD CLAY & SONS, LIMITED, BUNGAY, SUFFOLK.

BY THE SAME AUTHOR

MENS CREATRIX. An Essay. 8vo. 10s. net.

CHRISTUS VERITAS. An Essay. 8vo. 10s. net.

CHRIST IN HIS CHURCH. A Charge. Crown 8vo. 3s. 6d. net.

THE KINGDOM OF GOD. Crown 8vo. 3s. net. Globe 8vo. 2s. net.

THE NATURE OF PERSONALITY. Crown 8vo. 3s. net.

THE FAITH AND MODERN THOUGHT. Six Lectures. Crown 8vo. 3s. net.

CHURCH AND NATION. The Bishop Paddock Lectures for 1914–15. Crown 8vo. 3s. net.

PLATO AND CHRISTIANITY. Three Lectures. Crown 8vo. 2s. 6d. net.

ISSUES OF FAITH. A Course of Lectures. Crown 8vo. 2s. 6d. net.

FELLOWSHIP WITH GOD. Sermons. Crown 8vo. 6s. net.

STUDIES IN THE SPIRIT AND TRUTH OF CHRISTIANITY. Sermons. Crown 8vo. 4s. 6d. net.

REPTON SCHOOL SERMONS. Studies in the Religion of the Incarnation. Crown 8vo. 4s. 6d. net.

LIFE OF BISHOP PERCIVAL. With Portraits. 8vo. 18s. net.

FOUNDATIONS. A Statement of Christian Belief in Terms of Modern Thought. By Seven Oxford Men : B. H. STREETER, R. BROOK, W. H. MOBERLY, R. G. PARSONS, A. E. J. RAWLINSON, N. S. TALBOT, W. TEMPLE. 8vo. 10s. 6d. net.

MACMILLAN & CO., LTD., LONDON

NEW & RECENT THEOLOGICAL WORKS

ADVENTURE: THE FAITH OF SCIENCE AND THE SCIENCE OF FAITH. By BURNETT H. STREETER, D.D., CATHERINE M. CHILCOTT, M.A., JOHN MACMURRAY, M.A., and ALEXANDER S. RUSSELL, D.Sc. Edited by BURNETT H. STREETER, D.D. 8vo. 7s. 6d. net.

HERBERT EDWARD RYLE, D.D., K.C.V.O., sometime Bishop of Winchester and Dean of Westminster. A Memoir. By the Rev. MAURICE H. FITZGERALD. With Portraits. 8vo.

STUDIES IN CHRISTIAN PHILOSOPHY. Being the Boyle Lectures, 1920. By W. R. MATTHEWS, D.D. Second Edition. Extra crown 8vo. 8s. 6d. net.

THE MAKING OF LUKE–ACTS. By H. J. CADBURY. Crown 8vo. 12s. 6d. net.

NEW STUDIES IN MYSTICAL RELIGION. The Ely Lectures, delivered at Union Theological Seminary, New York, 1927. By RUFUS M. JONES, D.D. Crown 8vo. 7s. 6d. net.

BUDDHISM AND ITS PLACE IN THE MENTAL LIFE OF MANKIND. By Dr. PAUL DAHLKE, Author of *Buddhist Essays*, etc. 8vo. 10s. 6d. net.

GREAT ENGLISH CHURCHMEN SERIES

EDITED BY SIDNEY DARK

Crown 8vo.   6s. net each

THOMAS ARNOLD. By REV. R. J. CAMPBELL, D.D.

ST. THOMAS OF CANTERBURY. By SIDNEY DARK.

THOMAS CRANMER. By Canon ANTHONY C. DEANE.

ARCHBISHOP LAUD. By REV. A. S. DUNCAN-JONES.

JOHN WESLEY. By the Very Rev. W. H. HUTTON, D.D.

MACMILLAN & CO., LTD., LONDON